The Sinclair [Management]

A step-by-step guide to the use of the electronic calculator in business

Christian de Lisle

A WOODHEAD—FAULKNER PUBLICATION

Woodhead–Faulkner Ltd.
7 Rose Crescent
Cambridge CB2 3LL

First published 1973

© Sinclair Radionics Limited/Woodhead–Faulkner Limited 1973

ISBN 0 85941 004 8

Conditions of sale
All rights reserved. No part of this publication may be
reproduced, stored in a retrieval system or transmitted, in any
form or by any means, electronic, mechanical, photocopying,
recording or otherwise, without the prior permission of the
publishers.

Printed in Great Britain by Galliard (Printers) Limited,
Great Yarmouth, Norfolk

Contents

Preface v

1. Introducing the Calculator 1
Controls. Number entry. Simple arithmetic. Chain calculation. Error correction. Constant arithmetic.

2. Percentages, Square Roots and Raising Numbers "to the Power of" . 8
Percentages. Square roots. Raising numbers "to the power of".

3. Calculations in Finance and Accounts . 16
Gross profit as percentage of sales. Gross profit as percentage of capital employed. Sales as percentage of capital employed. Sales as percentage of fixed assets. Sales as percentage of stocks held. Sales per employee. Profits per employee. Simple interest. Compound interest. Investment ratios. Gross yield %. Dividends. Earnings yield. Price/earnings ratio. Rights issues. Share values. Gearing. Net asset values. Amortisation. Hire purchase and the true rate of interest. Redeeming a short-term loan. Liquidity. Break-even point. Administrative costs. Average weekly wages. Work in progress and stock turnover. Project evaluation using discounted cash flow and annual cost methods. Inflation. Inflation accounting. Discounting—trade discounts and bills. Some useful calculations with a 10% VAT factor.

4. Calculations in Purchasing and Stock Control 50
Raw materials and bought-out-parts costs. Discounts for early payment. Overdue orders. Quality of goods.

Stock turnover. Stock turnover rate. Average age of stock. Cost of holding stock. Economic order quantity. Optimum number of orders. Lead time.

5. Calculations in Production 58

Factory on costs. Labour/unit costs. Use of a company's assets to the fullest value. Maintenance costs. Batch production quantities. Depreciation. Equipment replacement using discount factors. Research and development. Measurement of job times. Time forecasting for network analysis. Slack time in network analysis. Assignment of machines. Quality control. Obtaining "means" or averages and standard deviation.

6. Calculations in Marketing and Sales . . 78

Advertising. Marketing assets. Invoices. Sales office costs. Home/export sales. Calculating size of sales force. Sales manager's ratios. Reps' remuneration. Agents. Forecasting by moving averages. Rate of return pricing.

7. Calculations in Personnel 87

Recruitment. Newspaper advertising. Cost of recruiting through advertisements. Cost of recruiting through agencies. Recruiting costs at £ per head per year. Training costs. Personnel turnover. Industrial relations. Productivity agreements.

Preface

I have derived great pleasure from using a Sinclair calculator during the preparation of this book, and it would be discourteous if I did not take this opportunity of thanking Sinclair Radionics Ltd. for all their assistance, and also my most forbearing and enthusiastic publishers.

Inevitably, with so many different and divergent types of training and management, no examples would be likely to relate to the knowledge and practice of all and every one of my readers. It was decided therefore that examples given would be simple, intended only to outline the calculator mathematics rather than to relate to any particular or specific applications. Some effort, however, has been made, in purely financial examples, to bring them in line with "going rates", but, even here, with interest rates changing so rapidly the reader may have to adjust his current thinking as he turns the pages.

Some of the most specialised management methods unfortunately have had to be omitted owing to the lack of space, and many of the explanations, for the same reason, curtailed. However, once the techniques described have been mastered, those executives wishing to delve into the more complex mathematical aspects of their particular work should find little difficulty.

Lastly, may I stress one point? Percentages and ratios are valueless on their own. They must be related, for example, to the firm next door, to a different unit of sales in another department, to turnover figures, or to whatever is appropriate. This may sound obvious—it is—but nevertheless it cannot be stressed too often, for ratio data properly analysed can be the foundation on which management takes the most far-reaching and vital decisions.

C. de L.

Note to the Reader

Sinclair Radionics Ltd., the leading European manufacturers of electronic calculators, produce a range of models suitable for use in many areas of business. For full details of the products now available please write to the head office at:

> Sinclair Radionics Ltd.,
> London Road,
> St. Ives,
> Huntingdonshire PE17 4HJ
> England

In the United States please write to:

> Sinclair Radionics Inc.,
> Suite 2801,
> 375 Park Avenue,
> New York,
> NY 10022

Acknowledgement

The publishers are grateful to the Controller of Her Majesty's Stationery Office for kind permission to include cartoons by Peter Kneebone which originally appeared in the CSO/COI booklet *Profits from Facts*.

chapter 1

Introducing the Calculator

This book is a condensation of present management practices in which a calculator can be used, and is designed to help the busy executive put more into his day by relieving him of the tedium of manual calculations. Thus freed he will be in a better position to step back once in a while to view his company or department without the usual urgent pressures upon him. He will have time, too, to apply more of the modern management techniques which so often go unused because of the manual computation involved.

Management ratios have become a recognised way of conveniently controlling the financial state of a company and by which the senior executives of a company can judge its overall performance. However, there are many other ratios available which will enable management to monitor the performance of individual departments within a company.

The calculations given in the text obviously vary in complexity, but a great deal of effort has been made to simplify the techniques as much as possible, and few of the calculations involve more than a minute or two of calculator operation.

The techniques used in this book are equally applicable to desk or pocket calculators and much depends of course on the location of the executive at the time of the calculation. While in his own office, a desk machine has obvious advantages, but when visiting colleagues, on the shop floor, in meetings, when travelling and at home, the pocket calculator comes into its own.

A simple four-function calculator ($+$, $-$, $\times$, $\div$) with a constant facility will handle all the calculations in this book.

However, some of the more complex operations would be done faster by machines with square root and memory facilities. The four-function machine is now selling at a price well within the budget of any company, and the price of the more complex machines is also dropping as the volume of production builds up.

On the other hand sizes are now relatively stable, these being largely dependent on the necessity of a usable keyboard and readable display. The thickness and weight of the calculator is all-important in a pocket machine and this is controlled by the size of the batteries used. To obtain a reasonable battery life (say, 10 hours plus) most manufacturers have to resort to large and heavy batteries. Happily the unique and patented battery conserving electronics of the Sinclair "Executive" allow hearing-aid batteries to be used, which reduce the thickness to 9 millimetres and the weight to 70 grammes, the smallest in the world.

Using a modern electronic calculator is very simple if it contains "full-flow arithmetic logic". This simply means that calculations can be entered into the calculator in exactly the same order as they are written on paper, and long chain computations do not have to be split in the middle with sub-totals. Such machines can be generally recognised by the fact that the (=) button is separated from the (+) and (−) buttons.

For those familiar with electronic calculator operation, the rest of this chapter may be omitted. For those as yet unfamiliar with the versatility of these machines there follows a brief resumé of the basic operations which form the backbone of any more complex calculations. The instructions are given with the Sinclair calculators in mind, but will apply equally to many other calculators. If in any doubt, consult the individual calculator handbook.

Controls
ON/OFF Always switch a pocket calculator off when not in use, even if only for a few minutes. This will increase battery life.

C	This has three distinct uses, all concerned with clearing the contents of the calculator. It must always be used immediately after switching on. Its other uses are explained later.
0 to 9 and ·	The ten digits and the decimal point are used for entering numbers. Following switch-on and C, the next button pressed must be one of these.
+ − × ÷	These are the operators and are used for adding, subtracting, multiplying and dividing numbers.
=	This is used to terminate calculations.
K	The constant button allows numbers to be stored for repeated use, so that they do not have to be re-entered.

Number entry

To enter the number 256 simply press the buttons 2, 5 and 6 in turn. The digits will enter the display from the right, but will move to the left when an operator or = is used.

To enter 17·62, press the buttons 1, 7, ·, 6 and 2.

To enter ·03 press ·, 0 and 3. A zero will automatically be inserted before the decimal point when the number moves to the left of the display since the decimal point cannot appear on the extreme left of the display.

If the decimal point button is used more than once during the entry of a number the decimal point will appear in the position indicated by its last use. This may be used to correct a decimal point entered earlier in a number than intended; but a decimal point entered too late in a number cannot be corrected in this way.

Simple arithmetic

Switch the calculator on, press C, and try the following examples by pressing the buttons in the order in which the digits and symbols are written down. If you make a mistake, press C and begin again.

$$13 + 46 =$$

The display should now show 59·000000. If you looked at the display during the calculation you will have seen that + resulted in the preceding number, 13, being accepted and moved to the left of the display and that = caused the preceding operator, +, to be applied to the two numbers available: 13 and 46. The same sequence of operations can be observed in these further examples (you can carry straight on from each one to the next).

$$23·2 - 16·1 = \quad \text{Result } 7·1$$
$$16·1 - 23·2 = \quad -7·1$$
$$3·2 \times 4 = \quad 12·8$$
$$111 \div 37 = \quad 3·$$

By carrying out these calculations in sequence you will have demonstrated that = completes one calculation and allows you to carry on to an entirely separate calculation.

Chain calculation
Try these calculations

$$17·2 + 3·5 + 6·6 = \quad \text{Result } 27·3$$
$$6·9 - 2·2 + 7·3 = \quad 12·$$
$$4 \times 5 \times 10 = \quad 200·$$
$$45 \div 5 \div 3 = \quad 3·$$
$$14 \times 3 \div 21 = \quad 2·$$
$$4·4 + 6·2 \times 3 \div 6 = \quad 5·3$$

In each case the first operator caused acceptance of the first number, and subsequent operators and = caused execution of the previous operator on the two numbers available, which at any stage are the number just entered and the previous result.

In the last example the calculation performed was

$$[(4·4 + 6·2) \times 3] \div 6$$

If $4·4 + [(6·2 \times 3) \div 6]$ had been required, the calculator sequence would have been:

$$6·2 \times 3 \div 6 + 4·4 =$$

If = is followed by a number the calculation will be terminated
and a new one started with the new number; but if it is followed
by an operator the calculation will continue exactly as if = had
never been used. The following are therefore equivalent:

$$4·6 - 3·2 \times 4 =$$

and

$$4·6 - 3·2 = \times 4 =$$

Hence, = can be used to form a partial result (1·4 in this case)
before deciding on the next operator.

Error correction

If an error is made while entering a number press C. This will
delete the incorrect number and also the preceding operator, if
any, which must therefore be re-entered together with the correct
number. Suppose $3·4 \times 4·62 =$ had been intended but that
$3·4 \times 4·5$ had been entered. Then $C \times 4·62 =$ will correct the
error and complete the calculation.

If an error in entering an operator is realised immediately the
correct operator should be entered. This will delete the incorrect
operator. Therefore, $5·2 \times \div 4 =$ and $5·2 \div 4 =$ will have the
same effect.

Constant arithmetic

The constant facility enables you to use the same number over
and over again without having to re-enter it each time it is
required.

Switch on, press C, and enter 3 = K.

Now press 6 +.

You should get the result 9. The calculation which has been
carried out is 6 + 3 = 9.

Now try

$$5 - (3) = 2$$
$$4 \times (3) = 12$$
$$12 \div (3) = 4$$

In each case, the result (2, 12 and 4) is as if 3 = had been added to the entries which were actually made.

If operators are used without preceding numbers the constant will be added to, subtracted from, multiplied by, or divided into, the number on the display:

$$C6 = K \quad 15 + \div \quad \text{evaluates} \quad 15 + 6 \div 6 = 3\cdot5$$

and

$$C6 = K \quad + + \times \quad \text{evaluates} \quad 6 + 6 + 6 \times 6 = 108$$

Sometimes, after using a constant, it is required to continue operating without the constant. In this case the constant must be cleared, which is done by pressing C, so that it is not used on every subsequent occasion that an operator is used:

$$C8 = K \quad 4 + \div C \times 6 \quad \text{evaluates} \quad [(4 + 8) \div 8] \times 6 = 9$$

The C after $\div$ is necessary to ensure that the following $\times$ does not cause a multiplication by the constant, but instead waits for the next number. The process of clearing the constant will also have cleared the partial result, 1·5, from the display, but the value is retained internally and can be operated upon by the following operator.

A result which has arisen from previous operations can be made into a constant. For example, $3 \times 2 = K$ is equivalent to $6 = K$.

Even a result which has been produced using a constant can itself replace that constant, provided that the latter is first cleared:

C3 = K	make 3 a constant
6 ×	multiply 6 by 3
CK	clear the constant 3, and make 18 the new constant

The second C in the above example will have cleared the partial result, 18, from the display. If you now press 13 + you will get the result 31 but if you had simply pressed + the result would have been 36 (18 + 18).

Summary

To enter a number as a constant, enter the number
followed by = K
To make a partial result into a constant press K
If the partial result was formed using a constant press CK

Errors

Errors made while using the constant facility should be corrected without using C as this would also clear the constant. If an error is made in entering a number, press any operator to complete the calculation, then enter the correct number and the required operator(s). If the wrong operator is entered press the complementary operator to restore the number displayed, and then the correct operator. (+ and − are complementary to one another, and × and ÷ form the other complementary pair.)

chapter 2

Percentages, Square Roots and Raising Numbers "to the Power of"

Before we deal with calculations in the various sectors of business we must cover the three following principles. The first two we shall need to apply throughout the book, and the third, although useful elsewhere, will be applied mainly in the chapter on Finance and Accounts.

Percentages

Percentages are an invaluable method of giving a quick ratio to save long explanations. To tell someone you sold your house for 25% more than it cost is clear to all without disclosing either the cost or sale figure. And with the advent of 10% value added tax even those most uninterested in mathematics need to apply their mind to percentages.

$$40 \text{ as a percentage of } 500 = \frac{40 \times 100}{500} = \underline{8\%}$$

$$15\% \text{ of } 500 = \frac{15}{100} \times 500 = \underline{75}$$

$$\text{If } 80\% \text{ is } 113{,}000,\ 100\% = \frac{100}{80} \times 113{,}000 = \underline{141{,}250}$$

$$\text{To check: } \frac{80}{100} \text{ of } 141{,}250 = \underline{113{,}000}$$

For calculations it is helpful to decimalise fractions of 100, *i.e.* percentage. For example, $5\% = 0.05$, $12\% = 0.12$.

Your company comparisons between 1972 and 1973 show:

Sales increases   £5343 (1973)   £4343 (1972)

To take a percentage of the difference:

$$£5343 - £4343 = \frac{£1000 \times 100}{£4343} = 23.0256\%$$

But a quicker method on a calculator is

$$[(£5343/£4343) \times 100] - 100 = 23.0256\%$$

Profits before tax ($\times$ '000)

£477 (1973)   £303 (1972) = 57.4% increase

Earnings per share

£3.14 (1973)   £1.41 (1972) = 122.7% increase

On a calculator, percentage working is simplified, especially since decimalisation. In order to be able to "percentage" rapidly it is necessary to know the quick methods of programming your calculator.

To add a percentage
The ordinary method of adding percentage uplift is

$$\text{Basic figure} \times \frac{\text{Percentage}}{100} = \text{Uplift}$$

$$\text{Basic figure} + \text{Uplift} = \text{Gross total}$$

Thus:

$$\pounds 400 \text{ with } 25\% \text{ uplift} = \frac{\pounds 400 \times 25}{100} = \pounds 100$$

$$\pounds 400 + \pounds 100 = \pounds 500$$

A quicker method, provided it is not necessary to know the uplift figure, is

$$\text{Basic figure} \times \left(1 + \frac{\%}{100}\right) = \text{Gross total}$$

$$\pounds 400 \times 1 \cdot 25 = \pounds 500$$

To deduct a percentage
This can be achieved by the above formula:

$$\frac{\pounds 400 \times 25}{100} = \pounds 100$$

$$\pounds 400 - \pounds 100 = \pounds 300$$

Or a quicker method on a calculator is:

$$\text{Basic figure} \times \left(1 - \frac{25}{100}\right) = \pounds 400 \times (1 - 0 \cdot 25)$$

$$= \pounds 400 \times 0 \cdot 75 = \pounds 300$$

A percentage uplift to a known figure

The retail selling price of an article comes to £400. If the "mark-up" was 25% what was the wholesale price? (Ignore VAT.)

$$\frac{\text{Retail price}}{\left(1 + \frac{\%}{100}\right)} = \text{Wholesale price}$$

Therefore

$$\frac{£400}{1\cdot 25} = £320$$

Check

$$£320 + 25\% = £320 \times 1\cdot 25 = £400$$

If given the uplift amount only (here £80) but knowing the percentage uplift (25%), find the wholesale price.

First find retail price which is

$$£80 \times \frac{100}{25} \quad (\text{or } £80 \div 0\cdot 25)$$

Now bring £320 to retail by raising 25%:

$$£320 \times 1\cdot 25 = £400$$

Thus:

$$£80 \times \frac{100}{25} \times 1\cdot 25 = £400$$

or, quicker on a calculator,

$$£80/0\cdot 25 \times 1\cdot 25 = £400$$

Tax

Assume the gross amount is £600 and tax is levied at the rate of 30%.

$$£600 \times 0\cdot 3 = £180 \text{ tax}$$
$$£600 - £180 = £420 \text{ net}$$

or

$$£600 \times 0\cdot 7 = £420 \text{ net}$$

Given tax is £180—

> Find gross amount   £180/0·3 = £600 gross
> Find net amount   £180 × 7/3 = £420 net

Given net amount is £420—

> Find gross amount   £420/0·7 = £600 gross
> Find tax   £420 × 3/7 = £180 tax

Given gross amount is £600—

> Find net amount   £600 × 0·7 = £420 net
> Find tax   £600 × 0·3 = £180 tax

In relation to the "percentage uplift" above, we could consider tax as a "mark-down". VAT is a percentage uplift—see Chapter 3, p. 49.

You will observe therefore that adding and subtracting a straight percentage and a percentage uplift are two different things. Before calculating, always give a moment's thought as to which type of percentage answers your requirement. £400 with a straight 25% reduction gives

$$£400 - (£400 \times 25/100) = £300$$

or

$$£400 (1 - 0·25) = £300$$

but

$$£400/1·25 = £320$$

and becomes with 25% added

$$£320 + £80 = £400$$

Square roots

An excellent short-cut method on your mini-calculator by which to find square roots without square-root tables or calculating with a √ key is obtained by a series of "approximations". Do not be put off by that word, for you will see the result is completely accurate. To obtain a square root on your calculator make a *rough guess*, as near as possible, as to what you think the root is likely to be (the nearer the guess, the less work you have to do!). Having made your guess, continue as outlined in the following example:

Find $\sqrt{133}$.

As $\sqrt{144}$ is 12, then guess 11.

$$133/11 = 12 \cdot 090909$$
$$\text{Add } 11 = 23 \cdot 090909$$
$$\div 2 = 11 \cdot 545454$$

(If your calculator has a K, then K this result.)

Repeat the above process, but replace 11 (your original guess) with your latest result, *i.e.* 11·545454.

$$133/11 \cdot 545454 = 11 \cdot 519685$$
$$\text{Add } 11 \cdot 545454 = 23 \cdot 065140$$
$$\div 2 = 11 \cdot 53270$$

Continue to repeat this process, each time substituting the denominator of 133 by the last result, until this result is repeated. That then becomes the square root.

Continuing the above process results in 11·532563.

Continuing once more results in 11·532563.

As this result is the same, then:

$$\sqrt{133} = 11 \cdot 532563$$

Check your result (always):

$$11 \cdot 532563 \times 11 \cdot 532563 = 133$$

Using a "Sinclair Executive", or other Sinclair machines, with their particular and rapid "K" function, the problem is perhaps most simply explained by a numerical example:

Find square root of 5.

First guess 2·2

$$\text{C. Enter } 2 \cdot 2 = K5 \div + C \div 2 = 2 \cdot 2363636$$
$$K5 \div + C \div 2 = 2 \cdot 2360679$$
$$K5 \div + C \div 2 = 2 \cdot 2360679$$
$$\sqrt{5} = 2 \cdot 2360679$$

Raising numbers "to the power of"

In the normal course of events raising to the power is not often required, and in cases where it is (see, for example, the section on compound interest in Chapter 3) in the old days lengthy log workings were necessary. Now, however, a calculator can rapidly achieve the same results and a simple method for calculating an annual compound interest sum is outlined below:

$$£1000 \text{ at } 9\tfrac{3}{4}\% \text{ for 20 years} = £1000 \times \left(1 + \frac{9 \cdot 75}{100}\right)^{20}$$

$$= £1000 \times (1 \cdot 0975)^{20}$$

Tap out 1·0975 multiplied by itself

$$20 \text{ times} = £1000 \times 6 \cdot 428218$$
$$= £6428 \cdot 22$$

Even so, if you were wise you double-checked in case you had over- or under-done the "times-multiplied".

But, supposing you required *monthly* compounding, the sum would be simple but the mechanics on your calculator more formidable, *i.e.*

$$£1000 \times \left(1 + \frac{9 \cdot 75}{1200}\right)^{20 \times 12} = £1000 \times (1 \cdot 008125)^{240}$$

Here you will need to tap out 1·008125 multiplied by itself 240 times and, apart from the time it would take, the room for error is extremely great. Unhappily, too, you will find four-figure logs will not be able to cope with 1·008125, and the nearest you will be able to find with four-figure log tables is 1·008. Eight-figure log tables are extremely hard and cumbersome to work out. What can one do? Can it be done on a calculator? The following is the most simple method.

Nearly every calculator, with or without a constant, can multiply a number by itself, *e.g.* $2 \times 2 \times 2 \times 2 \times 2 = 32$, and this is often done by merely pressing the $\times$ key continually, *i.e.* in other words the method of "tapping out" mentioned above.

Mathematically $(1·008125)^{12 \times 20} = (1·008125)^{240}$ and is the same as $[(1·008125)^{20}]^{12}$

So to find

$$(1·008125)^{240} = 6·974$$

on your calculator raise

$$(1·008125)^{20} = 1·175676$$

and now raise

$$(1·175676)^{12} = 6·974$$

The accuracy of the decimal places, over three places of decimals, will depend on the digit capacity of your individual calculator, for raising with the power of 240 is a fairly substantial rise—in fact nearly a 600% increase!

If you had an uneven number, say, $(1·008125)^{297}$, all you would do would be to find two "multipliers" which give a figure near to the one by which you are raising, *e.g.*

$$29 \times 10 = 290 \, (297 - 7) \quad \text{or} \quad 17 \times 17 = 289 \, (297 - 8)$$

$(1·008125)^{297}$ can then be calculated by

$$[(1·008125)^{29}]^{10} \times (1·008125)^{7}$$

or

$$[(1·008125)^{17}]^{17} \times (1·008125)^{8}$$

which both equal 11·06.

chapter 3

Calculations in Finance and Accounts

In this chapter the terms used are in such general currency that it is hardly necessary to define them initially, and this will be done only when necessary in particular sections. Doubtless each reader will know full well how to calculate his own sales per annum, fixed assets and the like. Admittedly auditors have their own views, often slightly divergent, on the more complex components of a Consolidated Balance Sheet, such as goodwill, reserves and net operating assets, but as these hardly lend themselves to ratio and percentage workings we need not dwell at length on them in this chapter.

The chapter begins with a few examples of ratios and percentages, all of which are simple to work out on a calculator. Readers, of course, will be able to supply many more, particularly allied to their own expertise and their own field.

Gross profit as a percentage of sales

Gross profit   £850,000
Sales   £4,000,000

$$\frac{£850{,}000 \times 100}{£4{,}000{,}000} = 21 \cdot 25\%$$

Gross profit as a percentage of capital employed

Gross profit   £850,000
Capital employed   £2,750,000

$$\frac{£850{,}000 \times 100}{£2{,}750{,}000} = 31\%$$

Sales as a percentage of capital employed
Sales £4,000,000
Capital £2,750,000

$$\frac{£4,000,000 \times 100}{£2,750,000} = 145\%$$

Sales as a percentage of fixed assets
Sales £4,000,000
Fixed assets £10,000,000

$$\frac{£4,000,000 \times 100}{£10,000,000} = 40\%$$

Sales as a percentage of stocks held
1200 TV sets are sold per year ex works at £100 per set and stocks held are 300.

$$\text{Sales as a percentage of stock} = \frac{300 \times 100}{1200}$$

$$= 25\%$$

This can be expressed as a turnover ratio

$$\frac{\text{Stock}}{\text{Sales}} = \frac{300}{1200}$$

$$= 0\cdot25$$

But if you take reciprocal $1/0\cdot25$ = turnover 4 times a year.
If you required days to turn over stock

$$\frac{300}{1200} \times 365 = \text{every } 91\cdot25 \text{ days}$$

Sales per employee
Sales   £1,000,000
Number of employees   1000

$$\frac{1000 \times 100}{£1,000,000} = 0.1\%$$

or £1000 worth of sales per employee.

Profits per employee
Profits   £100,000
Number of employees   500

$$\frac{500 \times 100}{£100,000} = 0.5\%$$

or $\frac{1}{2}\%$ per profits to workforce, giving a ratio of 2 (1/0·5) or £200 of profits per employee.

Simple interest
£500 at 10% simple interest is £500 × 10/100 = £50 interest.

£500 × (1 + 10/100) = £550 capital, with interest.

For 10 years (simple interest), future value is

$$(£50 \times 10) + £500 = £1000$$

or, alternatively

10% × 10 years = 100% in 10 years

$$= £500 \times \left(1 + \frac{100}{100}\right) = £500 \times 2$$
$$= £1000$$

i.e.   = £500 capital + £500 interest

Compound interest
As all readers will know, this means that the interest for one year is added to capital and the interest for the following year and subsequent years is levied upon "capital with interest added".

£100 at 10% compound interest for 5 years is thus:

$$£100 \times 1 \cdot 1 \times 1 \cdot 1 \times 1 \cdot 1 \times 1 \cdot 1 \times 1 \cdot 1$$
$$£100 \times (1 + 10/100)^5 = £161 \cdot 05 \text{ future value}$$

or

$$£100 \times (1 \cdot 10)^5 = £161 \cdot 05 \text{ future value}$$

Now all percentages in terms of interest are considered to be on a "per annum" basis. If the above had been monthly, the future value would have been

$$£100 \times \left(1 \times \frac{10}{12 \times 100}\right)^{5 \times 12} = £164 \cdot 53 \text{ future value}$$

or

$$£100 \times (1 \cdot 008333)^{60} = £164 \cdot 53 \text{ future value}$$

Here you will see that although the interest was termed the same, 10%, because the compounding was for monthly periods the future value increased by nearly £3.50 over the 60 months (5 years). But, consider, if the future values for monthly compounding are different to the future values for annual compounding, the interest rates, being on a "per annum" basis, must also be different. In other words what is the correct, or "*effective*" annual interest rate if we take the monthly future value? What we really want to find out is what is the interest rate at annual compounding, not monthly, which will bring the future value to the same amount as we produced by compounding monthly.

A simple method on your calculator is to take the 10% and convert this to a 12-month basis as follows:

$$\left(1 + \frac{10}{1200}\right)^{12} = 1 \cdot 104713 = 10 \cdot 4713\%$$

Thus we have found that 10% is the given, or nominal, rate per annum but if the compounding is monthly then the "effective annual rate" of interest is 10·4713%.

Quarterly compounding would be

$$\left(1 + \frac{10}{100 \times 4}\right)^4 = 10.3813\%$$

Please remember carefully the difference between nominal (simple), nominal (compound) and "effective annual" rate, for these factors often arise whenever interest rates are considered.

In case you ever need it, in reverse so to speak, to bring the effective annual rate to the nominal (compound) rate for monthly steps the above sum done in reverse looks like this:

$$\left[\left(1 + \frac{10.4713}{100}\right)^{1/12} - 1\right] \times 1200 = 10\%$$

Unless you have exponent facilities on your calculator you will not be able to raise numbers to the power of a fraction. If you find it necessary to do this, look at it another way and use logs, $^{12}\sqrt{\log 1.04713}$, which becomes:

Log $1.104713 = 0.043249 \div 12 =$ Antilog 0.003604
Standard number $= 1.0083333$
$(1.0083333 - 1) \times 1200 = 10\%$

Investment ratios

When considering yields, earning yields, price/earnings ratios and the like we must remember that in the United Kingdom (unlike, for the most part, in the United States) each equity share has a nominal value. For example, ICI has an ordinary nominal price of £1 whereas Imperial Group has 25p.

Gross yield %

$$\frac{\text{Gross dividend (in pence per share)} \times \text{Nominal price of share (p)}}{\text{Market price of share (p)}}$$

$$\frac{15p \times 25p}{98p}$$

$$= 3.83\% \text{ gross yield p.a.}$$

Dividends

If a company had an ordinary-share-issued capital of £8,727,000 (£1 nominal) and paid out dividends *gross* (that is the net amount to shareholders plus the tax on that amount to the Revenue by way of imputing the shareholders' tax as an offset against advanced corporation tax) of £567,255, the dividend per share would be

$$\frac{£567,255 \times 100}{£8,727,000} = 6\cdot5\text{p}$$

(The 100 in the equation is to bring the £ to pence.)

Supposing, however, the nominal value of the shares had been 25p, with 8,727,000 shares issued capital would have been

$$£8,727,000 \times 25/100 = £2,181,751 \text{ only}$$

In that case

$$\frac{£567,255 \times 100}{£2,181,750} = 26\% \text{ dividend}$$

Now let us see how to bring dividend percentages to pence, and the reverse.

$$\frac{\text{Dividend in pence} \times 100}{\text{Nominal value}} = \%$$

$$\frac{6\cdot 5\text{p} \times 100}{25\text{p}} = 26\%$$

$$\frac{\text{Dividend \%} \times \text{Nominal value}}{100} = \text{pence}$$

$$\frac{26\% \times 25\text{p}}{100} = 6\cdot 5\text{p}$$

Obviously when shares are £1 nominal (100p) the percentage and pence are the same.

Earnings yield

In the same way as dividends in pence per share divided by market price times the nominal share price equals dividends gross yield %, so also do the earnings yield calculations after having found the earnings per share:

$$\frac{\text{Earnings per share} \times \text{Nominal value}}{\text{Market price}} = \text{Earnings yield \%}$$

We shall return to this shortly.

In the old days, before April 1973, when the imputation system of corporation tax came into effect, one could divide earnings yield % by dividend yield % to obtain the time the dividend was "covered" by earnings.

Times covered under the imputation system is always calculated at maximum dividend payout.

But let us take some simple figures as an example and go through the imputation system in very general terms.

Profit before tax	£1000
Corporation tax	50%
Income tax	30%
Capital	£2000 (£1 nominal)
Price on market	350p
Ordinary dividend gross	£300
Preference dividend gross	£100

$$\text{Times covered} = \frac{\text{Profits before tax}}{1\cdot4} - (\text{"Less items"})$$
$$\times \frac{1}{\text{Ordinary dividend (gross)}}$$

$$\left[\left(\frac{£1000}{1\cdot4}\right) - £100\right] \times \frac{1}{£300} = 2\cdot05 \text{ times covered}$$

("Less items" are preference dividends, minority interests, etc.)

The factor 1·4 shown as dividing the "Profits before tax" is most useful but may need a short explanation. It applies only when corporation tax is at 50% and personal tax rate is 30% (see data above). It has been generally agreed that dividend cover will be calculated as if all profits were distributed as dividends, *i.e.* maximum possible dividend distribution. In that event, taking £1000 as profits before tax, the profits after tax become profits after corporation tax of 50% has been deducted: £1000 − £500 or £1000 ÷ 2 = £500 profits after tax. This £500 if distributed as gross dividends will need to be grossed up by dividing by 0·7 (50% tax rate), *i.e.* £500 ÷ 0·7 = £714·30. So (£1000 ÷ 2) ÷ 0·7 = £1000 ÷ 1·4 = £714·30.

Dividend yield %

$$\frac{\text{Dividend (p) per share} \times 100}{\text{Market price (p)}} = \text{Gross yield \%}$$

$$\frac{£300 \text{ (gross div.)}}{£2000 \text{ (share capital)}} \times 100 \text{ (to bring to p)}$$

$$= 15\text{p dividend per share}$$

therefore

$$\frac{15p \times 100}{350p} = 4 \cdot 29\%$$

In a like manner we could get the earnings yield provided we knew the earnings per share.

Earnings per share

$$\text{Eps} = \frac{\text{Retentions} + \text{Ordinary dividend (net)} \times 100 \text{ (to bring to p)}}{\text{Shares issued (ordinary)}}$$

Retentions
The data are:

Number of shares	2000
Profits before tax	£1000
Preference dividend	£100
Gross ordinary dividend	£300

A small table will probably clarify the imputation tax system better than a long explanation:

Profits before tax		£1000
Corporation tax	£500	
Less Advanced corporation tax preference dividend	30	
Less Advanced corporation tax ordinary dividend	90	380
Profits after tax		620
Less Preference dividend		100
Available for ordinary dividend		520
Ordinary dividend (gross)		300
Retentions		£220

$$\text{Earnings per share} = \frac{[£220 + (£300 \times 0 \cdot 7)] \times 100}{2000} = 21 \cdot 50p$$

Earnings yield
This equals:

$$\frac{21\cdot50p \times 100}{350p} = 6\cdot14\%$$

compared to a gross dividend yield of 4·29%.

In the old days 6·14/4·29 would give a times covered of 1·43. But we know, having discovered it previously, that times covered was 2·05. We can get this answer by *grossing* up the earnings *yield* % (with full decimalisation)

$$6\cdot14/0\cdot7 = 8\cdot77\%$$
$$8\cdot77/4\cdot29 = 2\cdot05 \text{ times covered}$$

Price/earnings ratio

The P/E ratio is, in short, the number of years required for the earnings to reach the market price. P/E is sometimes called the year's purchase ratio or the earnings multiple, and can be found from the following formula:

$$\frac{\text{Market price (p)}}{\text{Earnings per share (p)}} = \text{P/E ratio}$$

and

$$\frac{350p}{21\cdot50p} = 16\cdot28 \text{ P/E}$$

A warning should be added here that the imputation tax system is a complicated matter, for when companies have foreign interests, and foreign tax, the whole tax structure reflects such interests. As a result times covered and earnings per share, and thus earnings yield and P/E, need to be adjusted accordingly.

The principles shown above are general ones only, and so care needs to be taken if individual companies, with their respective tax structures, are analysed.

Incidentally a P/E is the reciprocal of the earnings yield % × 100:

$$\frac{1}{16\cdot28} = 0\cdot061425$$

$$\times 100 = 6\cdot14 \text{ earnings yield \%}$$

Therefore given the P/E (as one often is in the financial press) one could accurately deduce the earnings per share.

$$\frac{\text{Price}}{\text{P/E}} = \text{Eps}$$

$$\frac{350\text{p}}{16\cdot 28} = 21\cdot 50\text{p Eps}$$

and

$$\frac{\text{Earnings yield \%}}{100} \times \text{Price} = \text{Eps}$$

$$\frac{6\cdot 14 \times 350}{100} = 21\cdot 50\text{p Eps}$$

Rights issues

More than often, companies give rights issues, which can be either issues to be purchased or issues given as a bonus, and the shares are on a ratio of the number of shares already issued and held by the shareholders.

XYZ Co. decides to give a bonus issue of one share per five shares held, *i.e.* 1 for 5 as it is, not unnaturally, called.

A shareholder owning some 5000 shares would receive $5000 \div 5 \times 1 = 1000$ shares.

A company making a bid for another company might offer seven of its own shares in return for five of the attacked company. A shareholder in the latter company owning 5000 shares would, if he accepted the offer, receive $5000 \div 5 \times 7 = 7000$ shares in the new company.

Recently a company decided to give a 1 for 25 bonus issue. A shareholder owning 1397 shares received 55·88 shares (1397 ÷ 25) by way of a certificate for 55 shares and a cheque for £2·64, *i.e.* the "difference". Why that particular amount?

The issue price of the share when the Stock Exchange authorities accepted the company's arrangements was 300p, *i.e.* each share issued free was equivalent to 300p. The shareholder therefore received 55 shares worth £3 each, *i.e.* £165 worth of bonus shares.

The 0·88 "difference" now had to be dealt with by the company.

The company reckoned that 88/100ths of the shareholder's holding was in effect

$$\frac{88}{100} \times 25 = 22$$

i.e. 22/25ths of a share. One share being worth 300p, then

$$\frac{22}{25} \times 300 = 264p \text{ or } £2.64$$

and the shareholder received a cheque for that amount at the same time as he received his new certificate for the extra 55 shares.

In fact, once one realises the method and reasoning one can simply multiply the "remainder" by the share price, *i.e.* 55·88 shares.

$$55·88 - 55 = 0·88$$

Multiply by share price

$$0·88 \times £3 = £2.64$$

Share values

The simple formula is as follows:

$$\frac{\text{Net assets}}{\text{Number of shares}} = \text{Value per 1 share,}$$

$$\frac{£120,000}{5000} = £24 \text{ per share}$$

not unusual in a small private company. If the Board recommended a "9 for 1" scrip issue the share structure would become

$$5000 + (5000 \times 9) = 5000 + 45,000 \text{ shares}$$
$$= 50,000 \text{ shares}$$

The new share value would then be £2.40 each.

Gearing

A company often has two types of capital structure. First, there are the fixed-interest stocks which are interest bearing at a fixed rate % per annum (usually paid half-yearly). Such stocks are secured by the assets of the company and in the event of liquidation are paid out before anything else, for indeed they are in reality secured loans. Hence the term, often used, loan stock.

The equity capital is the ordinary share capital which is risk bearing in that in the event of failure the ordinary shareholder can lose his entire investment. But the equity holder benefits from a company's success by increased dividends or bonus share issues. If the public see a good future in a company they purchase the equity shares and, with more buyers than sellers, the price rises.

The gearing of a company is the ratio or relationship between fixed-interest-bearing stock and equity shares. In the United States "gearing" is called "leverage".

$$\text{Capital gearing} = \frac{\text{£ loan stocks}}{\text{£ ordinary share capital}}$$

$$\frac{£500,000}{£2M} \times 100 = 25\% \text{ gearing}$$

Another company might have

$$\frac{£100,000}{£3M} \times 100 = 3\cdot3\% \text{ gearing}$$

Alternatively you could "gear" with

$$\frac{\text{Debenture loans}}{\text{Preference shares} + \text{Ordinary shares}}$$

But care must be taken when comparing companies, for as yet there are no specific standards laid down in company annual accounts to say exactly which interest-bearing stocks are above or below the line and you will also realise that deferred preference shares or convertible preference shares (*i.e.* convertible into ordinary shares) due to convert on a (sometimes) indefinable date in the future can play havoc with analysis.

Furthermore loan stocks pay their interest "before tax" whereas preference shares pay tax after profits have been calculated. All these factors can weigh when calculating gearing.

Another, therefore useful, ratio can be

$$\frac{\text{Earnings before tax}}{\text{Fixed interest charges p.a.}}$$

Say

$$\frac{£500,000}{£70,000} = 7 \text{ times}$$

(£70,000 being the annual interest on a $9\frac{1}{2}\%$ debenture loan of nearly £740,000).

Net asset values

When purchasing a share, or when considering the possibility of a "takeover bid" and attempting to assess the possible value of the bid, the "net assets" (the whole "worth" of the company from a balance sheet aspect) are an important factor.

$$\frac{\text{Net assets}}{\text{Number of ordinary shares issued}} = \text{Value of each share}$$

A company's net asset value is £3,128,000 and the value of the issued equity is £206,250. The shares are worth a nominal value of 25p. The number of 25p shares therefore is

$$\frac{£206,250 \times 100}{25} = 825,000 \text{ shares}$$

$$\frac{£3,128,000}{825,000} = £3.79 \text{ per share value}$$

Amortisation

There are several formulae for this important and necessary calculation, all resulting in the same answer, different only in their transposed form. However, it is to be recommended that the one given here should be used, for it is the easiest for use on a simple calculator (with no "memory" or "constant" facility) and necessitates the least amount of writing down of the intermediate results from your read-out—and, the less you have to annotate, the less possibility is there of error arising.

The formula for annual and/or period payments is

$$C \times \left(i + \frac{i}{(1 + i)^n - 1}\right) = \text{Payments } \textit{annually}$$

$$C \times \left(\frac{i}{m} + \frac{i/m}{(1 + i/m)^{n+m} - 1}\right) = \text{Payments } \textit{monthly}$$

where: C = capital or loan
i = interest as a percentage, *i.e.* $5\% = 0.05 = i$
n = number of years
m = monthly payments, *i.e.* $n = 12$

(For quarterly or half-yearly payments m becomes 4 or 2 respectively. If you think of n as "periods" of payment, then do not forget that the i must be divided by the factor by which you are multiplying the n years.)

We will now fill in figures so that we can visualise what the formula looks like—then we will go through the motions on your simple, inexpensive no-facilities calculator. (Those calculators "with facilities" make the calculations just that much quicker.)

Example 1. £1000 loan over 10 years at 5%.

$$\text{Annual payments} = £1000 \times \left(0.05 + \frac{0.05}{(1.05)^{10} - 1}\right)$$

$$= £1000 \times \left(0.05 + \frac{0.05}{1.628895 - 1}\right)$$

$$= £1000 \times (0.05 + 0.079505)$$

$$= £129.50$$

Example 2. As above but with monthly payments.

$$\begin{aligned}\text{Monthly payments} &= £1000 \times \left(\frac{0{\cdot}05}{12} + \frac{0{\cdot}05/12}{(1 + 0{\cdot}05/12)^{10 \times 12} - 1}\right) \\ &= £1000 \times \left(0{\cdot}004167 + \frac{0{\cdot}004167}{(1{\cdot}004167)^{120} - 1}\right) \\ &= £1000 \times \left(0{\cdot}004167 + \frac{0{\cdot}004167}{1{\cdot}647009 - 1}\right) \\ &= £1000 \times (0{\cdot}004167 + 0{\cdot}006440) \\ &= £10{\cdot}61 \end{aligned}$$

Having read the section on interest rates, nominal and effective, you will appreciate the reasons why if you divide the annual payments (£129·50) by 12 the result (£10·79) will not equate with the correctly calculated monthly payments (£10.61). Please refer also to the section on "Raising to the power of" on a simple calculator (see p. 14). To raise by 20 for 20 years is not difficult on a simple calculator but to raise to the power of 120 (for 10 years' 12 monthly payments) is both laborious and prone to error. It is recommended that you follow the method discussed by raising the number first to the 10th power and then that resultant by the further power of 12.

Let us now work right through a more difficult example on the simplest of calculators, having no frills or facilities other than straight $\times \div + -$ on the keyboard, but assuming that yours, like most calculators, can multiply one number by itself, *e.g.* $2 \times 2 \times 2 \times 2 \times 2$.

Example 3. £1000 for 20 years with monthly payments at $9\tfrac{3}{4}\%$.

The first thing to appreciate is that as there are monthly payments $9\tfrac{3}{4}\%$ will need to be divided by 100 and 12. Do so and *write down the result,* leaving the figures on the calculator "read out" thus:

$$9{\cdot}75 \div 100 \div 12 = 0{\cdot}008125 \quad (\textit{write down})$$

Plus 1 = 1·008125.
Now raise $(1·1008125)^{20}$ = 1·175676.
Raising this, $(1·175676)^{12}$ = 6·973525.

Referring, mentally, to the formula, 1 must now be subtracted:

$$6·973525 - 1 = 5·973525 \quad (\textit{write down})$$

After a time, you will not need to write down the whole formula or all the figures, but as we are starting we will in this instance:

$$100 \times \left(0·008125 + \frac{0·008125}{5·973525}\right) = \text{Monthly payments}$$

Some calculators with a "recall" (or reverse) key enable the operator with 5·973525 on his read-out to key in 0·008125, press the recall, press the divide and read out the answer. With a simple calculator this is not possible, which was why you were advised to "write down 5·973525" above.

Now key in

$$0·008125 \div 5·973525 = 0·001360$$

(add)

$$+ 0·008125 = 0·009485$$

(multiply)

$$\times 1000 = £9·49$$

The above method has required writing down only two figures, 0·008125, initially (and referring to it twice for keying in), and 5·973525 (and keying in once).

Hire purchase and the true rate of interest

An HP loan of £400 is serviced by a payment of £20 per month over 2 years. At the end of 2 years both the capital, originally borrowed, and the interest thereon have been repaid. The loan is then fully redeemed.

£20 for 24 months = £480
Deduct loan of £400 = £80 *interest* over 2 years
Interest over 1 year = £40
£40 as a percentage of £400 = 10% (nominal)

Thus 10% is the nominal (simple) interest rate and on the face of it looks an attractive rate of interest, compared with the present-day "going rates". But is it?

In fact what the borrower is doing each month is to pay his interest charges and repay his capital. Each month, by his capital repayments, his loan, period by period, is diminishing so that, say, in the twenty-third month's payment his capital is practically all repaid—*but* the interest continues to be at 10% on the original £400 loan.

It is clear therefore that the real or *true* rate of interest must be a good deal higher than the nominal 10%. What, in fact, is it?

The amortisation formula to find this rate has already been covered. Suffice it to say here that if you multiply the nominal rate by the factor 1·8 (10 × 1·8 = 18%) you will have very nearly found the correct "true" rate of *annual* interest. But this loan was for 24 months, *i.e.* payments were on a monthly basis. Therefore to be both accurate and correct we must bring this to a true "effective annual rate" which we discussed earlier.

$$\left(1 + \frac{18}{1200}\right)^{12} = 19 \cdot 56\%$$

In fact properly computed, by the correct formula, the *exact* rate is 19·75% so that we were not far wrong. So in general terms for monthly repayment to reach a fairly reasonable answer you can *double* the nominal (simple) interest HP rate to obtain what you are really paying in interest charges over each year, *i.e.* the "true effective annual rate %".

Redeeming a short-term loan

Sometimes it is desirable to "get out" of an HP or similar short-term loan before the final date is reached. With capital and interest mixed up in monthly payments how does one determine how much is fairly due to the lender?

The formula given below is generally acceptable in business for a short-term, reasonably unsubstantial, loan—for higher and longer types of mortgage loans the correct amortisation redemption formula must be employed. In the loan in the example there is not more than a 90p difference (the "correct" amount being 89p less than we are going to calculate below).

Let I = "interest charge", total interest on whole loan (£80)
T = number of remaining instalments (9 months to go)
N = number of total payments over 2 years (24 months)
P = payments per period (£20)

Supposing we wished to "get out" after 15 months' payments, *i.e.* with 9 months only to run. How much would it cost us to redeem the £400 loan?

$$PT - \left(I \times \frac{T(T+1)}{N(N+1)}\right) = \text{Redemption amount}$$

$$£20 \times 9 - \left(£80 \times \frac{9 \times 10}{24 \times 25}\right)$$

$$£180 - \left(£80 \times \frac{90}{600}\right)$$

$$£180 - £12 = £168$$

Liquidity

This is, in effect, the solvency of a company. To calculate this, the following ratio should be used:

$$\frac{\text{Annual assets (or gross working capital)}}{\text{Liabilities (loans, overdrafts, creditors)}}$$

£2M/£750,000 = 2·67 liquidity ratio

The ratio gives a general view of the security of a firm to its short-term creditors.

Annual assets of course are not fixed assets; admittedly in liquidation both annual and fixed assets are realised but fixed assets, in such circumstances, are not always quickly realisable and indeed may well not find their full value.

Liquid assets are made up of cash, value of debtors (trade and others), investments, stocks of new materials held and work in progress.

The "cash value" of debts (in the event of liquidation) cannot be taken at their face value and it is usual to deduct a percentage, *i.e.* what the banks or a factoring discount house would charge to "discount" the equivalent "bill".

Say

    £15,000 cash
    £21,000 debts (£25,000 debts discounted at 15%)
    £12,000 new materials
    £18,000 stocks in hand

    ———

    £66,000

    ———

£66,000 (assets)/£30,000 (liabilities) = 2·2 ratio

Break-even point

The break-even point is where sales are such that, at a given amount, there is neither profit nor loss.

A company has sales of 100,000 units per year with each unit selling for £1 and each unit costing 75p to produce. Capacity costs are £15,000. (Every company has costs appropriate to itself for establishing its present capacity, setting up the factory, tooling up, initial administrative costs, etc. These are called "capacity costs".)

Let C = Total capacity costs (£15,000)
    S = Unit price sold (£1)
    V = Unit production cost (75p)

$$\frac{C}{S - V} = \text{Break-even point}$$

$$\frac{£15,000}{£(1 - 0·75)} = 60,000 \text{ units sold to break even}$$

Administrative costs

These are not always covered in "overheads" although they fall under the overheads category. Administrative costs are costs incurred which are not in fact profit bearing and include telephones, Telex, window cleaning, heat, fuel, light in administrative offices (power in a workshop might well be included in production costs), staff parties and the like.

It is valuable to see how different costs such as wages, administrative costs, rental costs and so on relate to each other especially on a period basis so that hidden rises in any particular department cannot creep up unobserved. These ratios can also be related to sales, gross profits, net profits, on costs and any other outgoings or income.

Suppose a firm has an annual wage bill of £30,000. With turnover of £100,000 and profits after tax of £15,000 the administrative costs (here general overheads) are £12,000. (These figures are taken, as so many are in this book, as illustrative and are not based on any particular commercial example.)

$$\frac{\text{Wages}}{\text{Administrative costs}} = \frac{£30{,}000}{£12{,}000}$$

$$= 2 \cdot 50 \text{ ratio or } 40\% \text{ administrative costs to wages}$$

$$\frac{\text{Turnover}}{\text{Administrative costs}} = \frac{£100{,}000}{£12{,}000}$$

$$= 8 \cdot 33 \text{ ratio or } 12\% \text{ administrative costs to turnover}$$

$$\frac{\text{Profits after tax}}{\text{Administrative costs}} = \frac{£15{,}000}{£12{,}000}$$

$$= 1 \cdot 25 \text{ ratio or } 80\% \text{ administrative costs to profits after tax}$$

Average weekly wages

The *average* weekly wage of 40 operatives comes to £38.50 and dependent on the number of weeks paid during the year the annual average wage per head is obviously £38.50 × 52 (say) = £2002. With 40 operatives the total wage bill per year will be

$$£2002 \times 40 = £80,080$$

As a percentage of a gross turnover of £500,000 the wage bill will be

$$\frac{£80,080 \times 100}{£500,000} = 16\%$$

Work in progress and stock turnover

Suppose in an accounting period the cost of goods manufactured by a company is £16,000 and in the same period the average value of stocks used in work in progress is £1500.

$$\frac{\text{Average stocks work in progress}}{\text{Cost of goods manufactured}}$$

$$\frac{£1500}{£16,000} = 0 \cdot 09375$$

If the accounting period was 3 months

$$0 \cdot 09375 \times 3 = 0 \cdot 28 \text{ months}$$
$$0 \cdot 28 \times 30 = 9 \text{ days approximately}$$

Therefore work in progress takes 9 days to pass through factory floor.

$$\frac{\text{Average stocks of new materials}}{\text{Cost of materials used}} \text{ (within accounting period)}$$

("Average" stocks taken over 1 year and divided to accord with accounting period.)

$$\frac{£25,000}{£100,000} = 0 \cdot 25$$

If accounting period is 3 months

$$0.25 \times 3 = 0.75 \text{ months}$$
$$0.75 \times 30 = 22.5 \text{ days}$$

23 days is the actual time materials are held in stock.

Rapidity of transfer from finished goods to supply can be calculated as a finished goods/turnover ratio

$$\frac{\text{Cost of sales}}{\text{Average cost of finished goods}}$$

Project evaluation using discounted cash flow and annual cost methods

When management looks into a new project it wants to determine whether it is viable or not. If someone brings to management a new idea, say, for marketing or a take-over bid situation, the seller of the idea, if he is wise, will outline the annual return or yield and/or the capital profit expected after so many years. Management will then compare yield against the cost of the idea and mentally review their own yield requirements and the rate % on which their normal expected yield is based. If the scheme provides a better yield than they normally expect then they are interested; if not, the project is rejected. How does management make a comparative analysis of what they expect against the project potential?

There are two well-tried methods, DCF and annual cost method, which will be explained shortly, but before then we must be clear about *present and future values*.

We have already discussed compound interest whereby a sum of money is placed on loan each year, the capital and annually resulting interest being again "on interest" for each succeeding year—and so on until the term of the loan is completed.

$$£10,000 \times (1.10)^{10} = £25,937.42$$

which means that a *present value* of £10,000 in 10 years' time at 10% annual interest will have a *future value* of £25,937.42.

Discounted cash flow

From the above example it is clear that a future value of £25,937.42 in 10 years' time, at 10% interest, will be worth £10,000 now, *i.e.* the future value has been "discounted" to the present time. This can be calculated by multiplying the future value by the "discount factor" (DF), which is the reciprocal of the compound rate of interest:

$$DF = \frac{1}{\text{Compound rate of interest}}$$

Using the above example:

$$DF = \frac{1}{(1 \cdot 10)^{10}} = \frac{1}{2 \cdot 5937} = 0 \cdot 3855$$

i.e. £25,937.42 × 0·3855 = £10,000.

As a further example, the discount factors for a compound rate of 15% over 1, 8 and 9 years respectively would be as follows:

$$1 \text{ year} \quad DF = \frac{1}{(1 \cdot 15)^{1}} = 0 \cdot 8696$$

$$8 \text{ years} \quad DF = \frac{1}{(1 \cdot 15)^{8}} = 0 \cdot 3269$$

$$9 \text{ years} \quad DF = \frac{1}{(1 \cdot 15)^{9}} = 0 \cdot 2843$$

Annual cost method

In the section on amortisation (p. 30) it was seen that a loan, or capital sum, at a rate % over a period of years would service annual even payments in which there was an element of capital repayment together with the annual interest on the capital outstanding. This amortisation of a loan or capital sum is the basis of the "annual cost method" of analysing projects.

Example:

If a car was purchased for £2000 and it was expected to last 10 years before being written off, it could be said that the depreciation was £200 per year. Add on £250 for tax, insurance, petrol, etc. and the total cost per year would be £450. But would it?

To calculate the *actual* cost of the car per year, to allow for interest and capital growth which the £2000 could be earning, it is necessary to apply the amortisation (or capital cost/recovery) factor:

	Years	Cash flow		Amortisation factor at 10%	Actual annual cost
Capital outlay	0	£2000	×	0·1627	£325.40
Running costs	1–10	£250			£250.00
				Total	£575.40

As a reminder, the amortisation factor (AF) at 10% over 10 years is calculated as follows:

$$AF = 0{\cdot}10 + \frac{0{\cdot}10}{(1{\cdot}10)^{10}} = 0{\cdot}1627$$

Using the above example, if the annual payments of £325.40 and amortisation factor were already known, it is possible to calculate the capital sum required by multiplying the annual payments by the "interest factor" (IF):

$$IF = \frac{1}{AF}$$

i.e.

$$IF = \frac{1}{0{\cdot}1627} = 6{\cdot}1462$$

i.e.

$$\text{Capital sum required} = 325{\cdot}40 \times 6{\cdot}1462 = £2000$$

Examples of project evaluation

Supposing it was decided to evaluate a project in which £20,000 would need to be invested with an annual return, or net cash flow, forecasted to be £6000 per year over 5 years, at an interest rate of 15%.

Using discounted cash flow the present value of the annual return of £6000 would be as follows:

Period	Net cash flow	Discount factor (15%)	Present value
1	£6,000	0·8696	£5,217.60
2	£6,000	0·7561	£4,536.60
3	£6,000	0·6575	£3,945.00
4	£6,000	0·5718	£3,430.80
5	£6,000	0·4972	£2,983.20
	£30,000		£20,113

The present value of the forecasted cash flow (£20,113) is greater than the intended investment which would therefore indicate that the project is viable.

Using the annual cost method the same result can be achieved more easily as follows:

Period	Net cash flow		Interest factor (15%)	Present value
5 years	£6000	×	1/0·298316	£20,113

It follows that the annual cost method is more useful than discounted cash flow when the net cash flow remains steady year by year. However, as the following example will show, only discounted cash flow can be used when the net cash flow fluctuates annually:

Period	Net cash flow	Discount factor (15%)	Present value
1	£2,000	0·8696	£1,739.20
2	£3,000	0·7561	£2,268.30
3	£8,000	0·6575	£5,260.00
4	£11,000	0·5718	£6,289.80
5	£6,000	0·4972	£2,983.20
	£30,000		£18,540.50

On this basis the present value of £18,540.50 is some £1459.50 less than the £20,000 which would need to be invested and so the project would not be viable; the money could be better invested elsewhere.

Inflation

Every company, we hope, has growth over the years, but how true is the growth? If £100 purchased 200 shirts in 1950 and only 100 in 1970 then after these 20 years £100 is only worth £50 "purchasing power of shirts" as compared to the beginning of the period.

Equally if a company's profits increase from £100,000 to £300,000 (a rise of £200,000) in 5 years but inflation (or the debasement of money) is, say, 25%, then the rise has not been 200% but only 150% true rise in terms of the money because each year there has been a 5% inflation increase and the £200,000 rise is worth only £150,000.

Government statistics give a price/indices factor for every commodity; there are Stock Exchange indices, cost-of-living indices, etc., and these can be related to the particular sum you are doing.

For example, in money terms, if a company had sales of £14 million in 1963 and sales of £25 million in 1968, the *company* index, taking 1963 as the starting point at 100, would be $25/14 \times 100 = 178 \cdot 57$ for the particular commodity in question.

If the sales of the company were in food, the retail food price index would give a useful comparison towards company growth related to commodity inflation. If the food retail index in 1963 was $104 \cdot 8$ we must now convert that to 100 base:

$$\frac{104 \cdot 8 \times 100}{104 \cdot 8} = 100$$

and so if the food retail index is $123 \cdot 2$ in 1968 then

$$\frac{123 \cdot 2}{104 \cdot 8} \times 100 = 117 \cdot 56$$

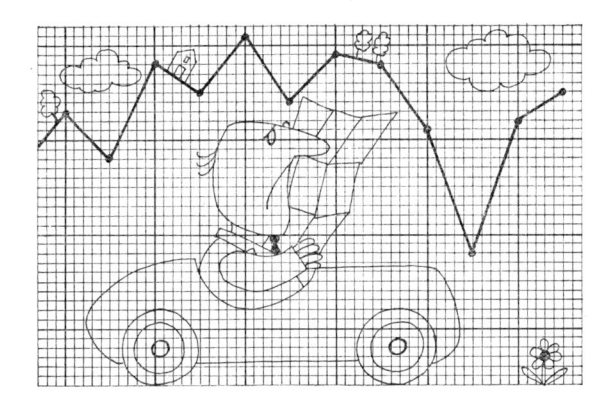

is the equivalent index (base 100) and this then is correctly in comparison to the company's 178·57 ratio (for we commenced the company's ratio at 100 in 1963).

In reality therefore the true index (not in money terms) is

$$\frac{178 \cdot 57}{117 \cdot 56} \times 100 = 151 \cdot 90$$

and this then can be suitably compared to comparative figures and an adjusted calculated index for other commodities this company sells such as drink or pharmaceutical drugs. (Government statistics will supply the necessary indices, by years, commencing at any base point which, as we have done above, must be brought to base 100 and the "final year index" so adjusted.)

Inflation accounting

Recently the Institute of Chartered Accountants have been considering ways and means by which all company accounts will reflect in some way the general inflation over the years, in the same way as we have shown above in relation to specific commodity indices.

This argument is very much in the news for accountants and analysts at the moment and there are many different suggestions as to how this cost-lift factor can best be inserted into a company's Profit and Loss Account.

The phrase "cost of living" may be clear to the man-in-the-street, but accounts-wise it raises many problems. Is the factor to be the consumer price index or the wholesale price index? Is depreciation to be inflated by the index or is normal depreciation to be shown but on assets revalued by the index? Cost of sales, stock holdings, turnover and operating costs will all be affected over a year; how is the index to be applied? Are "financing charges" to be inflated by the index or are they to be ignored in fixed interest rates?

All these questions are in the melting-pot and doubtless will take some time to be resolved before we all have a set accounting procedure for a cost index factor. But, when we do, it will have quite an impact on share values, earnings per share and, thus, comparative P/E ratios.

Property shares will doubtless benefit accounts-wise, for the property value index is likely to outstrip the cost-of-living (for want of a better term) index.

Whereas heavy industry, with massive re-investment problems, will, in the early days, be adversely affected, management, perhaps a little sceptical in the early days, may well realise, as we do now in our private lives, that it is probably sensible to "do it now" (re-tool or paint one's house) rather than to "wait a few years". Inflation cost accounts will thus highlight the necessity for even more careful consideration as to the ever-present and important "when"....

Discounting

We have already realised when dealing with DCF that a "bird in the hand...". Cash in the hand can often be more usefully employed than locked up in investments at a fixed rate, especially if you need to pay bills. Someone owes you £500 and is not required to pay for 3 months; you are being pressed to pay an urgent bill of your own for £400. How to raise the money? One way is to "sell" your "bill" (which you are owed but which you will not get for 3 months hence) *now*, for "a bit less than it is really worth". How much less?

Before going into the mechanics of bill discounting, which is a very simple matter, we must remind ourselves of two types of interest/percentage.

Simple interest
£500 at 6% per annum is

$$£500 \times \frac{6}{100} = £30$$

For two years this would be either

$$£30 \times 2 = £60$$

or:

$$£500 \times \frac{6 \times 2}{100} = £60$$

Present worth (compound interest)
There are two sorts of discount and we must be clear, initially, why they are different. Elsewhere (Discounted Cash Flow, p. 39) and in everyday life we are made aware that in compound interest

$$\text{Present value} \times (\text{Interest rate \%})^n = \text{Future value}$$
$$£100 \times (1 \cdot 05)^5 = £127 \cdot 63$$

which means that a present value of £100 in 5 years' time, compounded at 5% per annum, will be worth in the future £127.63. Often occasions arise when we wish to know what £127.63 in the future would be worth now, if the above circumstances, 5 years at 5%, obtained. In that case obviously it would become the above sum in reverse:

$$\frac{£127.63}{(1 \cdot 05)^5} = £100$$

That, for want of a better term, we shall call present-value discounting and it has nothing to do with bill discounting. Let us now pass on to consider trade discounts.

Trade discounts

If you enter a shop and ask the price of some goods, the salesman may well say to you that he will give you "a 10% discount for cash", meaning that if you pay a £10 bill "by cash" he will take off £1.

In our section on percentages (p. 8) we saw that

$$£100 + 5\% \quad \text{was} \quad £100 + \left(\frac{5 \times 100}{100}\right) = £105$$

and

$$£100 \times 1·05 = £105$$

were the same thing. But

$$£100 - 5\% = £100 - \left(\frac{5 \times 100}{100}\right) = £95$$

was not the same thing as

$$£100 \div 1·05 = £95·238$$

the difference being that

$$£95 \times 1·05 = £99·75$$

and

$$£95·238 \times 1·05 = £100$$

In getting a future value to a present value, *i.e.* a large amount to a smaller amount, the trade or banker's discount method is a percentage of the future value *subtracted* from the future value, whereas the true or present value discount is the future value *divided* by the percentage concerned.

Take, for example, £500 (FV) discounted for 1 year at 10%.

Trade or banker's discount £500 − (500 × 0·10) = £450
True or PV discount £500/1·10 = £454·55

To save all complications, therefore, bill discounting is always done at simple interest and by the trade or banker's method of discounting—so we can forget all other methods such as compounding and true discounts.

One final item before delving more deeply into discounting bills. Supposing you received £85 for a piece of furniture sold at an auction and knew the auctioneer had taken a 15% fee. If you wished to find out what the article had "fetched" in the auction room you could not calculate £85 × (15/100), for this interest increase would show an *untrue* £97·75 (or £85 × 1·15 = £97·75). Here, rather like bringing a tax net figure to gross, you find the difference between 100 and the percentage rate.

$$\frac{100 - 15}{100} = \frac{85}{100} = 0.85$$

£85 × $\frac{1}{0.85}$ (or 85 ÷ 0·85) = £100 auction price

In the same way as above, if you know the "bill" had cost the banker £492·50 and required to know the amount he would receive in 3 months' time, when the rate of the bill was 6%, you could *not* calculate

$$£492·50 + \left(£492·50 \times \frac{6 \times 3}{1200}\right)$$

equalling an *untrue* £489·87. But you would find the percentage rate for 3 months

$$\frac{6 \times 3}{12} = 1·5$$

$$100 - 1·5 = 98·5$$

Then
$$\div 100 = 0·985$$
and
$$£492·5 \div 0·985 = £500$$

Bills

If you are owed money for the sale of an article which will be paid in 3 months you can do one of three things: hold the bill yourself and receive the cash (or "face value") for the debt in 3 months' time; endorse the bill (debt) to someone else (perhaps someone to whom you yourself owe money); or "sell" the bill to a "banker" for an amount less than the "face value". This last method is called "discounting the bill". How does it work and how does one calculate the lesser amount (or discount amount) you will receive instead of the bill's (or debt's) face value?

In the first place the time factor is calculated *in days* to avoid the problem of 31- and 30-day months or leap years. There is a period of "three days' grace" for payments. Obviously this three days' grace does not arise if you keep the bill yourself, for there is no interest arising, but if you decided to "sell" your bill it is unlikely that you would arrange it on exactly the same day as you sold your original article.

You are owed £500—and the debt should be paid in 90 days, face value £500. The date of the bill is the date the debt is to be paid. Visualise a cheque, which is in reality a bill of exchange on your bank—a bill of exchange is the same thing worded, perhaps, somewhat differently. A bill would show the date it was drawn, the days to payment and the face value. Thus £500, 1st January 1974, for 90 days will mean that the bill is worth £500 on 31st March (no leap year). On 12th February you decide to sell to a bank for cash. The bill then has from 12th February to 31st March plus three days to run, *i.e.* three days plus 47 days. The banker decides the discount rate is 6%; therefore the sum will be calculated thus:

50 days. 6%. Face value £500.

$$\frac{£500 \times 50 \times 6}{365 \times 100} = £4\cdot 11 \text{ discount amount}$$

£500 − £4·11 = £495·89 discount value

You will receive £495·89 and the banker will receive £500 on 31st March. Out of interest, the banker's "rate of return" is

6·05%, fractionally greater than the going rate of 6%, because:

$$£495·89 \times x\% = £500$$

$$x = \frac{500}{495·89} = 1·008288$$

$$- 1 = 0·008288 \text{ (now adjust for days)}$$

$$\times 100 \times 365 \div 50 = 6·05033 = 6·05\%$$

or the "percentage uplift", adjusted to the year,

$$£500 - £495·89 = £4.11$$

$$\left(\frac{£4·11 \times 100}{£495·89}\right) \times \frac{365}{50} = 6·05\%$$

Banking practice in the United States is to work on a 360-day year basis and in that case the above discount would be £4·17 and discount value £495·84 provided their current practice was a three days' grace period. If not 47 days = £3·92 and £496·08.

Some useful calculations with a 10% VAT factor

If the retail price of an article was £156, with VAT at 10%, the price to a purchaser would be £156 + £15·6 = £171·60. If you had columns of input or output prices and needed further VAT data the following rules may be of use. The most useful "factor" is 11 (for a 10% tax) obtained thus:

$$(1 + 10/100) \times (100/10) = 11$$

Conversions
  (i) Retail price to purchase price = £156 × 1·10 = £171·60
 (ii) Purchase price to retail price = £171·60/1·10 = £156
(iii) Purchase price to VAT   = £171·60/11   = £15·60
 (iv) Retail price to VAT   = £156 × 0·10   = £15·60
  (v) VAT to purchase price   = £15·60 × 11   = £171·60
 (vi) VAT to retail price   = £15·60 ÷ 0·1 = £156

(If VAT was 8%, 1·08 × (100/8) = 13·50 factor.)

chapter 4

Calculations in Purchasing and Stock Control

Raw materials and bought-out-parts costs

It is often important to management to relate raw materials to the final cost of the units being sold and to other factors relating to production costs, sales and administration.

Let us take a small company making TV sets. About the only outside "bits and pieces" which it purchases from outside manufacturers (bought-out parts) are the cathode-ray tube and some switches and lead cables. The remaining raw materials are made up in the factory itself. The wholesale price of the unit is £100, and the mark-up was 25% on total production costs. The labour accounted for £20 per unit, the bought-out-parts cost was £25, and the raw materials purchased were £35.

Useful ratios would be

$$\frac{\text{Raw materials cost}}{\text{Production cost}}$$

$$\frac{\text{Bought-out-parts cost}}{\text{Production cost}}$$

and

$$\frac{\text{Raw materials cost} + \text{Bought-out-parts cost}}{\text{Production cost}}$$

For example, using our above figures, the last ratio (as a percentage) would be:

$$\frac{£35 + £25}{£80} \times 100 = 75\%$$

If the factory was making other articles besides TV sets, *e.g.* heaters and washing machines, it might be useful to find the ratio between the total bought-out-parts costs and other factors, and in that case it would merely be a matter of finding the bought-out-parts costs per unit, adding the different types of unit and dividing by the factor required in the ratio, whether sales, production, labour or mark-up.

Discounts for early payment

Cash discounts can be given by manufacturers to their retailers as an inducement to pay their bills promptly.

Terms could be, for instance, $2\frac{1}{2}\%$ discount if bills were paid within 14 days. A bill for £500 would then be £500 − (£500 × 2·5/100), namely £487·50, a saving of £12·50 for early payment.

Another method, often used in the United States, is the "10% n/60", meaning that a 10% discount will be allowed on 60 days payment if the bill is paid within that period. The "n" here stands for "net".

$$(£500 \times 10/100) \times 60/360 = £8·33$$

(The United States works on a 360-day basis for discounting.)

Overdue orders

Our TV manufacturer usually holds 100 tubes in stock, replacing them by 50 per month. Each tube costs £20, so that stocks held would be worth 100 × £20 = £2000. There being a rumour that delivery was likely to be delayed several months, to be on the safe side a further 250 tubes were ordered immediately and they were delivered before the delays occurred. Delivery recommenced normally after 4 months.

We need hardly dwell on the high costs that the company would have incurred if the production manager had not shown the foresight he did. The very minor cost of £55 to the company due to the slight dislocation from the normal batch ordering can be seen below.

Normal supply of tubes is 150 over 3 months and is worth £3000. 250 tubes cost £5000, which is £2000 in excess of estimates and the normal arrangements made for payment financing. Normal overdraft facilities at the bank are running at a rate of 11%. Therefore £2000 × 0·11 × 3/12 (for 3 months) = £55. Each unit therefore cost £55/150 = 37p in "charges". Each unit normally costs £20, therefore the cost for those 3 months is £20·37.

Another way of working out the cost is

$$£(3000 + 55)/150 = £20·37$$

Quality of goods

Quality is reflected in rejects or returns due to failure or unacceptance. If for example in a period of 12 months your firm supplied some £5500 worth of goods to a specific order and in that period £440 worth were returned for not being within sufficient tolerances, the percentage rejected would be £440 × 100/£5500 = 8%, and a critical look should be given to the quality control department. Either a base figure for comparisons could be laid down arbitrarily by management or an average reject ratio could be taken over a period of years or months. But however it is arranged it is essential to know whether one is running above or below quality average.

Stock turnover

When considering the financial aspect of stock turnover, stock held should be considered at cost.

If a firm had stock-taking in December and it was estimated that £20,000 stock was held and it was also known that replenishment stocks of £7500 by the end of March (90 days) had occurred, a ratio between these two facts can be made:

$$\frac{£20{,}000}{£7500} \times 90 = 240 \text{ days}$$

This is an average of 240 days' purchase which is "invested" in the balance of the total stock held. And if of this £20,000 stock held some £5000 of this was raw materials, then a comparable ratio could be found.

$$\frac{£5000}{£7500} \times 90 = 60 \text{ days}$$

And if the firm in question had a basis of paying its bills every 3 months you might care to consider that there was probably a connection between delayed payment and raw material ratio.

Stock turnover rate

It is obvious that the one thing to avoid is any particular item of stock remaining on the shelf too long and out of proportion to other items held. A quick turnover of stock enhances profitability, turning raw materials rapidly into final product sales. Considering the movement of raw materials we could evaluate this by the cost of materials which we have used against the average amount of raw material stock we hold. This average can be calculated annually, monthly, quarterly, etc.

Of one item

$$\frac{\text{Material used cost}}{\text{Raw stocks held (average)}}$$

For example:

$$\frac{£20,000}{3000} = 6.67$$

which is the ratio during the accounting period.

If the accounting period under review was for 4 months then divide the ratio

$$\frac{4}{6.67} = 0.6 \text{ months}$$

and 0·6 × 30-day month becomes 18 days. Thus 18 days become the number of days that particular item of stock was shelf held.

Average age of stock

Overdrafts are expensive, and, even if a company can finance itself, the more stocks held idle mean the more finance that is either locked in or interest paying.

The average age of stock can be evaluated as

Days in accounting period $\times \dfrac{\text{Amount held at beginning of accounting period}}{\text{Amount of purchases during same period}}$

This represents the average day's purchase invested in total stock balances.

$$\frac{5000}{3000} \times 90 = 150 \text{ days}$$

Sometimes a manufacturing process takes longer than others and it may be difficult to turn over stocks held. In these cases a careful watch should be kept on the optimum items held and ordered.

Cost of holding stock

Books have been written about this subject, and the methods of alleviating the cost, and so in such a short space it is unlikely to be covered fully. Briefly, however, costs of holding stock arise from many factors, rent of premises, insurance, heat, light and water, wages, spoilage and depreciation, and interest on capital locked up.

Suppose a company's stock holding is assessed at £100,000 per year. If this money was invested at 10% it would produce £10,000 in the same way that if one has to borrow this money to pay stock-holding costs at the same rate it would cost £10,000. If the firm's operating profit was 25%, lowering the cost of stock holding would substantially increase profits.

Annual cost of holding stock × Interest rate/100 will equal the *value* of the cost of holding stock. Stock control therefore is a matter of cost benefit analysis and everyone should consider stock holding as an "investment" and balance the "return" against other investment avenues and opportunities.

Economic order quantity

One of the best ways of keeping stock-holding costs to a minimum is to evaluate carefully the economic amount of materials ordered. Suppose a firm making TV sets and selling 100 a month requires a certain part worth 25p. What is the economic batch order?

In the first place the firm decided to hold in store some 50 parts and it expects a return on sales of 2% per month. In that case the capital tied up would be £0·25 × 50 × 2/100 = 0·25, called the "stock-holding cost". We also know that with each "batch order" the administration, labour and other costs come to £4. These are called "ordering costs". Working on a unit basis, if orders are increased by batches the ordering costs will diminish and the unit stock-holding costs will increase.

To find the EOQ, the formula is as follows:

$$\text{EOQ} = \sqrt{200 \times \frac{\text{Sales} \times \text{Ordering costs}}{\text{Cost per item} \times \text{Rate of return}}}$$

Thus

$$\text{EOQ} = \sqrt{200 \times \frac{100 \times £4}{£0 \cdot 25 \times 2}}$$

$$= \sqrt{160{,}000}$$

$$= 400$$

Optimum number of orders

Taking the last example, we found the EOQ on 100 sales per month to be a lot order of 400.

A useful ratio is

$$\frac{\text{Sales per month}}{\text{EOQ}}$$

which in this case would be 0·25.

If we multiply this ratio by 12 months, we get the optimum number of times we should order in a year, in this case every three months (12 × 0·25).

If we had been considering weekly sales, and our figures were adjusted accordingly, the ratio would have been the same, giving us: 0·25 × 52 = 13 weeks.

Lead time

This is a term denoting value of orders outstanding as a ratio of the daily (or monthly) value of the purchases.

If a company is selling 100 TV sets per month it needs to purchase 1200 chassis per year. Each chassis costs £10. Suppose delivery of the chassis was delayed and the value of the uncompleted order was £4000 outstanding. How many months will be required to fulfil the order?

$$\frac{\text{Value of orders outstanding}}{\text{Value of monthly purchases}}$$

$$\frac{£4000}{100 \times £10} = 4 \text{ months}$$

Alternatively

$$\frac{\text{Value of outstanding orders}}{\text{Purchases already received/Number of months so far gone}}$$

$$\frac{£4000}{£8000/8} = 4 \text{ months}$$

This ratio could also be applied to supplier's reliability.

chapter 5

Calculations in Production

The infinite variety of production lines makes it unsound to generalise, yet impossible to particularise. The techniques of production of individual companies will mean that there will be, inevitably, a large number of personal yardstick ratios that each production manager will swear by and that will cause him to discount any others.

However, management, irrespective of the type of production line, must know certain data, and without such information no check can be kept on production, its method and results, and no decisions can be taken.

The main requirement of management is to obtain the lowest production costs for the maximum sales potential. But sales value relative to production could by itself be misleading, for the company's resources, the back-up to production, have a vital part to play.

These resources, or assets, range from factory premises to the fork-lift trucks, plant, machinery vehicles, stock of raw materials and finished goods, together with work in progress. Let us call them production assets.

If we took the sales value of production, which we mentioned above, and subtracted the production costs, we could call this, overall, the production contribution and this management ratio would then be

$$\frac{\text{Sales value of production} - \text{Production costs}}{\text{Production assets}}$$

which could be refined to

$$\frac{\text{Production contribution}}{\text{Production assets}}$$

But there is no reason why production costs cannot be related to other factors—and, indeed, they should be, *e.g.*

$$\frac{\text{Production costs}}{\text{Sales}}$$

Production costs are comprised of raw material cost, bought-out-parts cost, direct labour cost and factory on cost. (These, apart from the last, are primary costs.)

Factory on costs

Every organisation, every company, has administrative overheads. So does every factory and every shop floor.

To digress for a moment, an organisation such as a local District Council, whose cost control is perhaps somewhat primitive, might well not have a breakdown of its overheads between general overall administrative costs and the overheads in its vehicle department. If a vehicle was hired from the Council to a smaller local organisation, the Treasurer, who would know the average cost per mile per vehicle and who also would have a general cost of depreciation of the vehicle, with insurance and so on, would quote a hire price, probably per mile. Just before doing so—to make certain the Council was not out of pocket—he would add on an arbitrary percentage as "on cost".

A well-run factory does not "add on a percentage" for on cost, for it knows, or should do, to a penny the cost of overheads within the particular factory or individual shop floor.

Thus costs relating to actual production area are separated from the general overhead costs of the company as a whole.

Therefore ratios such as Factory cost/Sales, On cost/Factory cost, and On cost/Sales can be extremely useful to management.

A company with

Raw materials cost	£20,000
Bought-out-parts cost	10,000
Labour cost	100,000
would have a prime cost of	£130,000
If factory on cost was a further	10,000
The total production costs would be	£140,000

If sales were £215,000, then

$$\frac{\text{Production costs}}{\text{Sales}} = \frac{£140,000 \times 100}{£215,000}$$

$$= 65\%$$

i.e. production costs were 65% of the sales, or sales to production costs were on a 1·54 ratio. And this ratio could be compared to a Sales/Total costs ratio.

$$\frac{\text{Factory on costs}}{\text{Labour costs}} \times 100 = \frac{£10,000 \times 100}{£100,000}$$

$$= 10\%$$

$$\frac{\text{Factory on costs}}{\text{Production costs}} = \frac{£10,000 \times 100}{£140,000}$$

$$= 7·14\%$$

$$\frac{\text{Factory on costs}}{\text{Prime cost}} = \frac{£10,000 \times 100}{£130,000}$$

$$= 7·69\%$$

If marketing and distribution was £25,000
and company total overheads (including factory on costs) were £20,000

total costs = £140,000 + £25,000 + £20,000 = £185,000.

$$\frac{\text{Sales}}{\text{Total costs}} = \frac{£215,000}{£185,000}$$

$$= \text{a ratio of } 1\cdot16$$

or a percentage of costs to sales of $16\frac{1}{4}\%$; this figure would be called a $16\frac{1}{4}\%$ profit margin.

Labour/unit costs

If 5000 TV sets were sold annually for £100 per unit, sales would be £500,000. If labour was £100,000 the labour cost per unit would be £100,000/5000 = £20, and the percentage of labour costs to sales would be

$$\frac{£100,000 \times 100}{£500,000} = 20\%$$

or

$$\frac{£20 \text{ per unit labour} \times 100}{£100 \text{ per unit sales}} = 20\%$$

If profit margin was 10%, the remaining cost per unit would be (£100/1·1) − £20 = £70·91 and the Labour/Costs ratio would be 20/70·91 = 0·28, making a percentage of labour to costs of 28%.

Another useful percentage is

$$\frac{\text{Overtime hours} \times 100}{\text{Basic hours worked} + \text{Overtime hours}}$$

Use of a company's assets to the fullest value

Operating assets are the value of money locked in for operating the company, *i.e.* value of factory space, warehousing, jigs, tools and any assets used in production. Such operating makes a profit and this *operating profit* is gross operating profit and is determined before any deductions of taxes or interest payments (*e.g.* leasebacks or warehousing). It does not include business profit from outside investment. However, depreciation for the years under review is deducted before calculating such profit.

There must be a balance between such profit and assets apart from the straight ratio Operating profit/Operating assets and this could well be Operating profit/Sales or Sales/Operating assets, which brings us on to the maximum use of assets, and in particular maximum use of factory space and machine tools, *i.e.* plant in relation to costs and finance.

$$\frac{\text{Output (actual)}}{\text{Output (maximum possible)}} = \text{Full utilisation ratio}$$

$$\frac{500{,}000 \text{ units (or £ worth)} \times 100}{750{,}000 \text{ units (or £ worth)}} = 66{\cdot}66\%$$

In other words the output and utilisation are operating only at 67% efficiency.

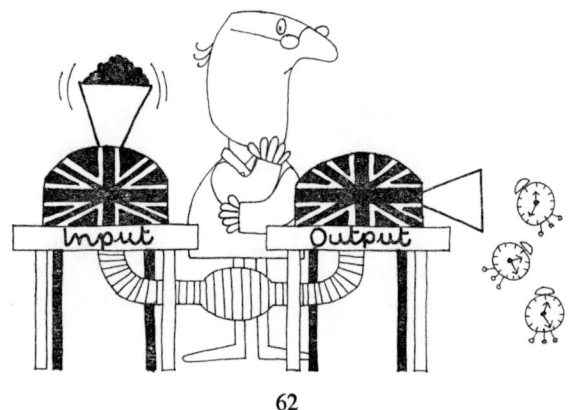

Whereas it is simple to determine actual output, "maximum possible output" is not just what your production manager would like it to be, or said it would be, if he received Board agreement to his latest project. In fact maximum output is actual output *plus* all the factors "mitigating against" full output. These could be strikes (nil working), time lost due to bad organisation of available work, machine breakages, or stoppages caused by machine maintenance and replacements or updating with latest modifications, machines running slow and to any other factors particular to an individual factory floor which slow up or lose production.

Maintenance costs

This is an area where, often, major cost savings can be made. It is essential therefore to know unit maintenance costs.

Suppose shop-floor maintenance costs £3000 per year and output is 5000 units per year

$$\frac{\text{Maintenance costs}}{\text{Unit of output}} = \text{Unit maintenance costs}$$

$$\frac{£3000}{5000} = 60\text{p per unit}$$

If each unit at point of sale costs £20 then maintenance is 3% of unit sale price, *i.e.* £0·60 × 100/£20.

Batch production quantities

It is assumed that the demand for, or usage of, the product being manufactured is constant, so that the effects of stockpiling are known. There are two different situations which may arise:

(i) The entire manufactured batch becomes available at the same time. In this case, the optimum batch quantity, *B*, which minimises the cost of setting-up plus stock holding, is given by the following formula:

$$B = \sqrt{\frac{2Md}{S}}$$

where M = setting-up cost per batch
d = demand for the product per unit of time
S = stock-holding cost per item per unit of time

(ii) The manufactured items become available continuously during the batch production period. In this case, the optimum batch quantity is given by:

$$B = \sqrt{\frac{2Md}{S[1 - (d/p)]}}$$

where p = number of items which are manufactured per unit of time.

Depreciation

The calculation, and the level of assessment, of depreciation is a necessary factor not only in accounting but also in any financial forecasting. There are several different methods which can be employed to find the depreciation and the method used normally becomes fairly obvious when the problem under review presents itself.

One method is to take an arbitrary percentage of depreciation per annum; another is to calculate the length of the life of the item together with its initial cost and residue value; and the third method, often used for property, is to divide the number of years into the original cost less the retirement value.

If we had plant worth £60,000 and we reckoned, from a book value point of view, that at the end of 50 years the plant would have a written-down value of only £10,000, the calculation would be £(60,000 − 10,000)/50 = £1000.

Taking the arbitrary percentage method, supposing we purchased a new piece of machinery for £10,000 and estimated that in the first place it would depreciate by 20% per year for the first 3 years and thereafter by 25% per year, we could draw up a table showing the annual depreciation (see p. 65).

This method, you will appreciate, gives the greatest depreciation in its earlier years, which may not be truly representative of what you require. Also it will be seen it takes a long time for this piece of machinery to be a complete write-off and in any event maintenance and modifications will probably affect its further "life". This will perhaps call for a reassessment of the percentage depreciation later.

TABLE SHOWING ANNUAL DEPRECIATION — Years 1-3 at 20%, following years at 25%

			Depreciation
End of year 1	£10,000 − (£10,000 × 20/100)	£8000	£2000
2	£8,000 − (£8,000 × 20/100)	£6400	£1600
3	£6,400 − (£6,400 × 20/100)	£5120	£1280
4	£5,120 − (£5,120 × 25/100)	£3840	£1280
5	£3,840 − (£3,840 × 25/100)	£2880	£960
6	and so on		

Supposing on the other hand you purchased a delivery truck for £2500 and you estimate that after 6 years its "scrap" or trade-in value will be £400. We now have to find the amount that it will depreciate annually so that at the end of the sixth year it would be worth exactly £400. How is this calculated?

First we find the value required for depreciation, which is £2500 less £400 = £2100. The "sum-of-the-digits method" could be used and here the years are 1–6. Add up

$$1 + 2 + 3 + 4 + 5 + 6 = 21$$

It is not very difficult to add this small amount of numbers on your calculator but it would have been an impossible labour if for example you had needed to add up 12 years over monthly periods, *i.e.* 1–144.

The tip is to always take the final figure, 6, add 1 to it, making 7, multiply 6 by 7 and divide by 2.

$6 \times 7/2 = 21$; $36 \times 37/2 = 666$; and having established the final sum of the digits in question it is now merely a matter of multiplying the item we wish to depreciate by the ratio of 1/21 to find the amount of depreciation per year, *i.e.* £2100 × 1/21 = £100 depreciation per year. A table would look like the first on p. 67. The £2500 − £2100 in depreciation over 6 years leaves £400 as salvage scrap or trade-in value.

An alternative method to this is to leave in the scrap value and to use the "double declining method". Take the declining factor of 2 and consider a 100% depreciation divided by the number of years' life. In the above example this would be $2 \times 100/6 = 33.33$. This becomes your "multiplier" (in effect the percentage decline per annum comparable to the earlier example where we depreciated £10,000 worth of machinery by 25% per annum) and using your constant you subtract, each year, 33·33% from your present book value.

Before you do this, consider a shortened method:

$$\frac{£2500 \times 33.33}{100} = 833.33 \text{ depreciation in the first year}$$

ANNUAL DEPRECIATION OF TRUCK — 1

	Book value (£)	Depreciation (£)	Value after annual depreciation (£)
End of year 1	2100	600	1500
2	1500	500	1000
3	1000	400	600
4	600	300	300
5	300	200	100
6	100	100	0

£2100 × 6/21
5/21
4/21
3/21
2/21
1/21

ANNUAL DEPRECIATION OF TRUCK — 2

	Book value (£)	Depreciation (£)	Value after annual depreciation (£)
End of year 1	2500 × 0·3̄3̄	833·3̄3̄	1666·6̄6̄
2	1666·6̄6̄ × ,,	555·55	1111·1̄1̄
3	1111·1̄1̄ × ,,	370·37	740·74
4	740·74 × ,,	246·91	493·83

But to arrive at 833·33 we found initially our 33·$\overline{33}$/100 × 2500. So in effect we have

$$\frac{£2500}{100} \times \frac{100 \times 2}{6} = \frac{£2500 \times 2}{6}$$

Each "factor" could thus be considered as 2/6 = 0·$\overline{33}$ and multiplying this by 2500 brings us back to 833·$\overline{33}$. On this basis a table would look like the second on p. 67. As the salvage value was £400 the depreciation in the fifth year would be only £93·83 (£493·83 − £400).

Lastly let us consider the case of your own car purchased at the beginning of 1970 for £2000. By the end of 1974 with a heavy mileage on the clock you are offered a trade-in value of £600. What exactly is the depreciation of your car over the 4 years in question? You could say that in the 4 years it has depreciated £1400 and therefore the annual depreciation is £350. Alternatively if you wanted to get a fair assessment of how it depreciated each year you could use the sum-of-the-digits method seen below.

In view of the well-known saying that as you drive a new car out of the showroom it drops £100 you may well consider the sum-of-the-digits method is the fairer in this instance.

Sum of the digits = 4 × 5/2 = 10
£1400 × 4/10   £560 1st year's depreciation
  ,,   × 3/10   £420 2nd ,,   ,,
  ,,   × 2/10   £280 3rd ,,   ,,
  ,,   × 1/10   £140 4th ,,   ,,

Supposing you decided to run the car for a further 2 years, reckoning that the value would not drop more than another £75. We would then have £2000 − £(600 − 75) = £1475 over 6 years.

Sum of the digits = 6 × 7/2 = 21
5th year's depreciation £1475 × 1/21 = 1 year's depreciation
  = £70·24

To get each year's depreciation on the car merely subtract 1 year's depreciation from each year commencing the first year.

£1475 × 6/21 = £421·43 (− 70·24) 1st year's depreciation
    = £351·19 ,, 2nd ,, ,,
    = £280·95 ,, 3rd ,,
    = £210·71 ,, 4th ,, ,, *
    = £140·47 ,, 5th ,, ,,
    = £70.28 ,, 6th ,, ,,
    = 0 ,, 7th ,, ,,

* Check at random

£1475 × 3/21 = £210·71

Equipment replacement using discount factors

The management of machines and their replacement is not covered between these pages, for it is a most technical subject and is not one that can be lightly touched upon.

However, replacement policy follows on from the sections on discounted cash flow and the use of discount factors (p. 39). Thus follows an example of how to use a financial formula for solving practical problems.

A piece of equipment costs originally £500, and repairs over 10 years are set out annually in a table (see p. 70). We want to discover in what year it would have paid the company best to replace that piece of equipment so that with this type of analysis available it can rethink its replacement policy.

The lowest weighted average gives the year of the lowest discounted cost, year 6.

A works manager would now doubtless take other machines and make comparable analyses. With several analysis reports the mean "best year" would be likely to show the optimum replacement year on which company policy could be based.

Research and development

Management can place an arbitrary percentage on profits or sales and allocate such funds to the R & D division. It depends

EQUIPMENT REPLACEMENT USING DISCOUNT FACTORS

1 Year	2 Annual repair costs (£)	3 Discount factor 10%	4 Discounted costs (£)	5 Principal + Σ discounted costs	6 Cumulative Σ D.F.	7 Weighted average (£)
1	0	1	0	500	1·0000	500
2	15	0·9091	13·64	514	1·9091	269
3	30	0·8264	24·79	539	2·7355	197
4	50	0·7513	37·57	577	3·4868	165
5	70	0·6830	43·46	620	4·1698	149
6	100	0·6209	62·09	682	4·7907	142
7	145	0·5645	82·00	764	5·3552	143
8	200	0·5132	102·64	867	5·8684	148
9	220	0·4665	102·63	970	6·3349	153
10	250	0·3855	96·38	1066	6·7204	159

(column 4 = column 2 × column 3)

Σ = the sum of.

Notes: Column 3 is discount factor produced either from tables or $1/(1\cdot1)^{n-1}$ for the nth year

4 is column 2 × column 3

5 is the original cost, £500, then column 4 added year by year

6 is 1 plus column 3 added year by year

7 is column 5 divided by column 6

Lowest weighted average (here year 6) is "best replacement year".

on the type of firm. Research is obviously more necessary in a company making drugs than one making Christmas cards. Research usually takes some time to filter through to sales before finally making an impact on profits. How can one best assess the ratios and percentages?

One could take sales of products developed and introduced over the past x number of years and divide that by the total sales. This would give you a "new market sales" ratio; or profits from the "new products" over the past x years over total profits.

Having calculated the above ratios they can be compared with the "firm next door" or with profitability of another range of goods which have been selling for some time, *i.e.* that range of goods which are about to become obsolete.

Another method is to find the *percentage annual growth.*

Assume that in 1968 profits were £100,000 and in 1973 £300,000.

$$\left(\frac{£300,000}{£100,000}\right)^{1/5} = 3^{1/5} = 1 \cdot 245731 \text{ growth ratio per year}$$
$$\text{or } 24 \cdot 6\% \text{ growth}$$

Supposing you took the median point (after $2\frac{1}{2}$ years, *i.e.* 5/2):

$$(\text{Growth ratio})^{\text{median point}} \times \text{First year profits} = \text{Median profits}$$
$$(1 \cdot 245731)^{2 \cdot 5} \times £100,000 = £173,205$$

But note this: $(3^{1/5})^{2 \cdot 5}$ is the same as $3^{(2 \cdot 5)/5} = 3^{0 \cdot 5} = \sqrt{3}$.
Therefore:

$$\sqrt{\frac{\text{Final year's profit}}{\text{First year's profit}}} \times \text{First year's profit} = \text{Median profit}$$

$$\sqrt{3} \times 100,000 = \text{Median profit}$$
$$1 \cdot 73205 \times 100,000 = £173,205$$

Then taking a percentage of your annual R & D costs, say £30,000:

$$\frac{£30,000 \times 100}{£173,205} = 17\cdot32\%$$

whereas an R & D percentage of your base year (£100,000) and of your final year (fifth) would give respectively 30% and 10% and, averaged here, would give you 15%.

On the whole the median method is to be preferred.

Measurement of job times

Measuring a job time is simply a matter of taking a number of observations and averaging the results, provided that precautions have been taken to eliminate possible causes of bias. Even so, the problem remains of how many observations must be taken. Suppose that it is required that the averaged time from observations shall have a 95% chance of being in error by no more than 5%. Then the number of observations which must be made is

$$40 \frac{\sqrt{n\Sigma(x_1)^2 - (\Sigma x_1)^2}}{\Sigma x_i}$$

where $n =$ number of observations in a pilot study, or the first n observations of the actual study

$x_1, x_2, \ldots, x_n =$ observed times

Note that 40 is always used as a standard factor in this formula.

Time forecasting for network analysis

Most network analysis techniques (Programme Evaluation and Review Technique (PERT), critical path analysis (CPA), etc.) depend upon the assumption that the time taken to complete a single activity will vary in accordance with a beta probability distribution.

Consequently, the best estimate of the duration of an activity is given by:

$$\frac{a + b + 4m}{6}$$

where a = optimistic estimate of the duration of the activity
b = pessimistic estimate of the duration of the activity
m = most likely duration of the activity

Note that $4m$ is always used as a standard factor in this formula.

The variance of the duration is best estimated from:

$$\frac{(b-a)^2}{36}$$

Slack time in network analysis

(i) The total slack time of an activity within a network is the amount of time in excess of its estimated duration which that activity may take to complete without increasing the overall time to complete the entire network of activities.
Total slack = Latest finish time − Earliest start time
  − Estimated duration

(ii) The free slack of an activity is the time by which its duration may increase without affecting the slack of any future activity.
Free slack = Earliest finish time − Earliest start time
  − Duration

(iii) The independent slack of an activity is the time by which its duration may increase without affecting the slack of any other activity in the network, either preceding it or succeeding it.

Only by studying the slack times of activities is it possible optimally to allocate excess resources of manpower and/or materials.

Assignment of machines

In certain types of production process a single person is required to operate or supervise the operation of several machines. The assignment of too few machines is obviously a poor use of labour resources, while the assignment of too many machines will result in machines being idle, awaiting the attention of the operator. Provided that all the machines which may be assigned to a single operator have identical characteristics, the arrangement which will minimise idle time is given by:

$$N = \frac{T + t_m}{T + t_o}$$

where N = optimum number of machines
T = total time during which both machines and operator are active
t_m = time during which the machines are active and the operator is idle
t_o = time during which the operator is active and one machine is idle

When the formula gives a value for N which is not a whole number, the next smaller or larger number should be taken according to the relative costs of operator and machines.

Quality control

Suppose that the acceptable proportion of defective items produced by a production process is p. Provided that reasonably large samples are taken at regular intervals, warning and action limits can be established from the following formulae:

$$\text{Warning limit} = p \pm \sqrt{\frac{p(1-p)}{n}} \times 1\cdot 96$$

$$\text{Action limit} = p \pm \sqrt{\frac{p(1-p)}{n}} \times 3\cdot 09$$

where n = number of items tested in the sample.

Note that 1·96 and 3·09 are always standard factors in these formulae.

When the proportion of defective items in a sample of n items exceeds the warning or action limits, appropriate action should be taken.

Obtaining "means" or averages and standard deviation

Arithmetic mean or average

Doubtless we all know, in general terms, how to calculate a batting average or the cost of several commodities purchased. The total number of runs are added and divided by the number of innings. The "average" is therefore the sum (which is designated by the Greek letter sigma, Σ) divided by the number of entries (n).

$$\frac{\Sigma x}{n} = \frac{6 + 8 + 4 + 12 + 9 + 10 + 10 + 9 + 7 + 5}{10 \text{ (entries)}}$$

$$= \frac{80}{10} = 8 \text{ average}$$

8 is the average number of runs made and is in fact the "mean" of the series of numbers above. The mean is often symbolised by $\overline{X}$ (X bar).

It so happens that sometimes comparisons between means are necessary and here we can come up against problems unless we are careful. Look at the next set of figures.

$$\frac{6 + 8 + 45 + 2 + 3 + 2 + 2 + 2 + 8 + 2}{10} = \frac{80}{10} = 8$$

Here you will see that with a different set of figures the mean is the same. With a batting average this does not matter, but suppose the figures represented the result of a consumer test for electric light bulbs made by two different manufacturers A and B. If the bulbs were used for 12 hours per day and the figures represented months' life we would immediately notice that because Company B had one bulb only that ran for an excessive number of hours (45) this masked the fact that at least 4 of the remaining bulbs ran for only a very short time. By seeing the full range of figures we realise that we should avoid the purchase of manufacturer B's bulbs. But if we had only been given the statistical mean we could have assumed that the two manufacturers had an equal "life" span. This shows how statistics can misrepresent some of the simplest facts on occasions. If we were explaining to someone else the above figures we could of course say that with the same mean Company A had a range from 4 (lowest) to 12 (highest) and Company B ranged from 2 to 45, but this is a cumbersome and statistically inconvenient method of expression.

Standard deviation

Seeking therefore a more positive definition we use the term "standard deviation", σ, and, while at first sight this may appear mathematically complicated, with a calculator it becomes relatively easy.

Standard deviation derives from calculating the "differences" between the series of figures under observation and is calculated as follows:

$$\sigma = \sqrt{\frac{\Sigma x^2 - n(\bar{X})^2}{n-1}}$$

where σ = standard deviation
  Σx^2 = sum of squares of figures under observation
  $\bar{X}$ = mean of the figures under observation
  n = number of items under observation

For example, let us return to the manufacturers A and B, mentioned earlier, and compare their respective standard deviations:

Company A

$\Sigma x^2 = 36 + 64 + 16 + 144 + 81 + 100 + 100$
$ + 81 + 49 + 25 = 696$

$\bar{X} = \dfrac{80}{10} = 8$

$n = 10$

$$\sigma = \sqrt{\frac{696 - (10 \times 8^2)}{9}} = \sqrt{\frac{56}{9}} = 2\cdot49$$

Company B
$\Sigma x^2 = 36 + 64 + 2025 + 4 + 9 + 4 + 4 + 4 + 64 + 4 = 2218$

$$\bar{X} = \frac{80}{10} = 8$$

$$n = 10$$

$$\sigma = \sqrt{\frac{2218 - (10 \times 8^2)}{9}} = \sqrt{\frac{1578}{9}} = 13\cdot24$$

We can now see that manufacturer A has a far smaller deviation factor and so its products are preferable to those of B.

chapter 6

Calculations in Marketing and Sales

In general terms management attempts to sell its most profitable lines to the maximum and to restrict marketing costs to the minimum. At the same time it uses the minimum assets possible to achieve the maximum profitability in sales.

Marketing contribution/Marketing assets is the ratio combining the above objectives.

Marketing contribution is sales less marketing costs.

Marketing costs include advertising, office costs for selling and sales, distribution costs, bad debts, discounts and warehousing if applicable.

Marketing assets include finished goods, debtors, cash in hand and any capital assets such as distribution vehicles if applicable.

Added to the above costs for sales we must not forget sales representatives and their costs, expenses, vehicles, etc., and, also, if sales are carried out by local agents, their added costs.

All the above costs and data can be brought to ratios or percentages against total sales, *e.g.*

$$\frac{\text{Advertising costs}}{\text{Sales}}$$

or

$$\frac{\text{Bad debts}}{\text{Sales}}$$

Bad debts of £7500 against a total sales of £250,000 is a ratio of

$$\frac{£7500}{£250,000} = 0\cdot03 \text{ ratio}$$

or 3% debts to sales.

If advertising costs were 25% of sales (£250,000), advertising would cost £62,500 (25/100 × £250,000) or a ratio of 0·25.

Advertising

Above we showed advertising costs as a ratio 0·25, but advertising costs have a time lag before they are reflected, we hope, as increased profits in the Profit and Loss Account. We should therefore consider relating the past advertising costs to future benefit, in a like manner as when considering Research and Development.

$$\frac{\text{Advertising costs for period a–b}}{\text{Sales for period d–e}} = \text{Time lag ratio}$$

Advertising costs in 1972, including those for a new sales advertising campaign between May and December, were £75,000 total. Sales for 1973–74 are £360,000.

$$\frac{£75,000}{£360,000} = 0·21 \text{ ratio}$$

If normal advertising costs were, as hitherto, £62,500, the sales campaign became a "special allocation" of £75,000 − £62,500 = £12,500.

If the normal annual sales increase was an average of 15% we would expect the 1973–74 sales to be £250,000 (1972) + 15% = £287,000. But true sales were in fact £360,000, *i.e.* £72,500 increase as a result of the extra £12,500 spent on special allocations.

$$\frac{£12,500}{£72,500} = 0·17 \text{ ratio}$$

This is a ratio of 17% for advertising to sales, which is an improvement over the normal, and thus this particular sales campaign could be considered a successful venture.

Marketing assets

Marketing assets consist of finished goods, in this example

£20,000, selling and distribution costs, £7500, and debtors, £30,000, with sales of £250,000.

$$\frac{\text{Sales}}{\text{Marketing assets}} = \frac{£250,000}{£20,000 + £7500 + £30,000}$$

$$= 4\cdot 35 \text{ ratio}$$

or 23% marketing assets to sales.

Invoices

Invoices or orders will produce a block amount of sales and so it is useful to relate sales to "£ per invoice".

$$\frac{\text{Sales}}{\text{No. of orders}} = \frac{£250,000}{3000} = £83\cdot 33 \text{ per order}$$

Admittedly this is merely an average but it is a useful management guide for comparison with previous years, or between month and month or salesman and salesman.

Sales office costs

Every business, according to its nature, will have varying office (sales) costs, but they will relate to the sales and orders of the particular firm in question.

$$\frac{\text{Sales office costs}}{\text{No. of orders}} = \frac{£25,000}{3000} = £8\cdot 33$$

Compare these with the invoices per order above, and you will find the ratio is £8·33/£83·33 = 0·10, *i.e.* the sales office costs in this example are 10% of annual sales.

Home/export sales

Exporting may or may not be fun as a politician once suggested, but, whatever it is, sales managers, dealing with home and export sales, will inevitably need considerable data at their disposal if they are to be competitive in foreign markets. Such detailed data are beyond thescope of this book, but nevertheless even those executives without computer data available can, with their calculators, keep well abreast of the general principles and their firm's export drive.

If a breakdown of home/export sales is to be maintained, as it must be, the simplest way to draw comparisons is by ratios.

$$\frac{\text{Home selling costs}}{\text{Home sales}} \text{ against } \frac{\text{Export selling costs}}{\text{Export sales}}$$

Our total selling costs may well be conveniently broken down into:

$$\frac{\text{Selling costs total}}{\text{Home sales}} \text{ against } \frac{\text{Selling costs total}}{\text{Export sales}}$$

The total Selling costs/Sales would be represented as follows:

$$\frac{\text{Home selling costs} + \text{Export selling costs}}{\text{Home sales} + \text{Export sales}}$$

Taking a small firm having sales of £125,000, by the value of the commodity sold the selling costs home/export are out of proportion, but the initial reaction to certain foreign markets has caused management some concern:

$$\frac{\text{Home selling costs}}{\text{Home sales}} = \frac{£25,000}{£100,000} = 0.25 \text{ ratio}$$

or 1 to 4 cost to sales

$$\frac{\text{Export selling costs}}{\text{Export sales}} = \frac{£12,000}{£25,000} = 0.48 \text{ ratio}$$

or 1 to 2 cost to sales

$$\frac{\text{Selling costs}}{\text{Sales}} = \frac{\text{Home selling costs} + \text{Export selling costs}}{\text{Home sales} + \text{Export sales}}$$

$$= \frac{£25,000 + £12,000}{£125,000} = 0.3 \text{ ratio}$$

or 1 to 3 cost to sales

With such data management can make comparisons of ratios after a period of time, suitably chosen, between lower export selling costs and higher export sales against a diminishing, or expanding, home market.

Calculating size of sales force

Marketing and selling mean people, people buying (in large numbers, we hope) and people selling (in the smallest possible number). But how small, without sales suffering, is a decision that is really at the nub of the sales manager's expertise. A large sales force may well sell an immense quantity of goods but when the day of reckoning comes it could be that the cost of sales is so high as to lower profit margins to such a degree that the whole operation becomes a loss maker, or that raising the price of the commodity to combat high costs forces the firm out of the market. Management's task is not to wait for the day of reckoning but to be constantly reviewing such data, comparing individual sales representatives' results and considering the expansion, or diminution, of the sales force.

The usual formula for calculating size of sales force is

$$\frac{\text{Call frequency} \times \text{Number of customers}}{\text{Average daily call rate} \times \text{Sales working days in year}}$$

Customers are those with specific orders or, equally important, order potential.

The sales manager must, by drawing either upon his experience or from past data available, calculate the working days of his sales force and categorise his customers.

Sales force working days could be calculated as 365 less: average sickness days 8, training days 5, conferences 5, meetings 10, weekends 100 (50 × 2) and holidays 14—a total of 142 non-working (sales) days leaving 365 − 142 = 223 working days for sales.

Customer categorisation may be a little more difficult, for a large customer with a permanent order may not warrant as many calls as a smaller customer, expanding rapidly, with considerable order potential.

Type of customer (spending per year)	No. of customers		Visits per year		Total visits
1. £5000	50	×	12	=	600
2. £2000–£4000	200	×	8	=	1600
3. £3000 with potential	100	×	12	=	1200
4. £1500 not likely to expand	300	×	4	=	1200
5. £1000–£2000	50	×	2	=	100

Total calls: 4700

From his records the sales manager considers that on average his sales reps can work on a basis of 6 calls a day:

$$\frac{\text{Total annual call frequency}}{\text{Average call rate} \times \text{Sales working days}}$$

$$\frac{4700}{6 \times 223} = 3\tfrac{1}{2} \text{ salesmen}$$

If we have four salesmen we have a little "call time" in hand for new customers. Checking, with 4700 calls required and 223 working days, gives 21 calls per day and with "$3\frac{1}{2}$" salesmen we have 6 calls per day. With 4 salesmen either we make only an average of $5\frac{1}{4}$ calls per rep per day or, as was intended, we can make $(4 \times 223 \times 6) = 5352$ calls overall. This gives us $(5352 - 4700)$, a potential of 652 calls for new customers, a matter of 163 "extra" by each of the 4 salesmen.

There is nothing particularly clever about the above mathematics. What is essential is the level-headed assessment by the sales manager of customer potential and the amount of *productive* work the reps can undertake.

Sales manager's ratios

The sales manager's experience and business acumen cannot be gained without relevant data and he will probably have a series of relevant ratios to suit his particular problems.

$$\frac{\text{Rep's remuneration} + \text{Expenses (including car, etc.)}}{\text{Number of calls made}}$$

$\frac{£3500 + £1000}{1500 \text{ calls}}$ (including car depreciation) $= £3$ per call made

(Reps can work either on a straight salary or on a part salary, part commission on sales basis, or again on a commission only, with or without company "back-up", such as car, travelling expenses, etc. There are an infinite number of variations usually dependent on the type of selling envisaged.)

$$\frac{\text{Number of orders obtained by reps}}{\text{Number of calls made}}$$

$$\frac{400 \times 100}{1500} = 26 \cdot 7\% \text{ of successful calls}$$

The comparisons between individual reps can be illuminating.

400 orders with 4 reps is obviously 100 orders, on average, per rep, but the value of the orders is of probably greater significance.

If the total value of the 400 orders was £1 million, then the average order was worth £2500.

The total number of calls made was 1500 and therefore *on average* each call produced £1,000,000/1500 = £666 worth of orders.

If salesman A with 120 calls produced £320,000 worth of business, how does he compare with the mean?

$$\frac{£320,000}{120} = £2666$$

as against a mean of £2500.

If each call averaged £666 worth of orders and each call cost £3, the percentage call cost/worth is 3 × 100/£666 = 0·45% or a ratio of 1 to 222.

Reps' remuneration

If the rep who turned in £320,000 worth of orders was on $\frac{1}{2}$% commission (overall, commission may well be worked on x amount for the first £50,000, decreasing as volume increases), this would be worth £1600. If his total remuneration, excluding expenses, was £3500 his basic salary would be £1900.

Agents

Again there are many permutations dependent on the amount of "back-up" from the parent company that is given or required.

Working, for example, on a $12\frac{1}{2}$% commission basis on sales, £350,000 sales would give a commission of £43,750.

But a sales manager, taking into account commission, back-up and other agents' expenses arising, would view it thus:

$$\frac{\text{Agent's fees, etc.}}{\text{Agent's sales}} = \frac{£75,000}{£350,000}$$

$$= 21\cdot5\% \text{ approx.}$$

Forecasting by moving averages

This method simply uses an average of the previous values of a parameter to estimate the next value. For example, expected sales figures might be calculated as an average of the actual sales figures for the previous 4 months. This could be expressed symbolically as

$$S'_n = \frac{S_{n-1} + S_{n-2} + S_{n-3} + S_{n-4}}{4}$$

If, however, the sales figures are showing any distinct trends, the method of moving averages will result in less accurate forecasts and a graphical method is to be preferred.

It is often useful to be able to calculate S'_{n+1} from S'_n when S_n becomes known. The relationship between the two values is as follows:

$$S'_{n+1} = \frac{S'_n \times 4 + S_n - S_{n-4}}{4}$$

Rate of return pricing

The percentage mark-up on the cost price of an item will determine the profit on total annual costs. Therefore, if the planned rate of return on capital employed and the rate of capital turnover are both known, the percentage mark-up on cost is

$$\frac{\text{Capital employed}}{\text{Total annual cost}} \times \text{Planned rate of return on capital employed}$$

For example, if the capital employed is £5 million, the total annual cost is £12 million and the planned rate of return on capital employed is 24%, the percentage mark up is

$$\frac{£5,000,000}{£12,000,000} \times 24 = 10\%$$

(24% of £5 million = £1,200,000. £1,200,000 × 100/£12,000,000 = 10%.)

chapter 7

Calculations in Personnel

Personnel or labour is the heart which beats in any company and therefore interest, integrity, enthusiasm and ambition are all important factors when choosing staff at whatever levels.

The costs of obtaining or recruiting labour can become a substantial part of a company's annual costs. Conditions met within the company can have considerable bearing on turnover of staff, with consequent increased costs if turnover is inordinately high.

Recruitment

Of the several methods of recruitment, advertisement is probably the most basic and most used, and the most rewarding. Care and great technical skill are employed in drafting advertisements both to attract replies, by explaining the advantages to be gained in answering the advertisement, and at the same time to zone the advertisement to the type of recruit required. If advertisements are badly drafted the rewards (the number of answers and applicants of the right calibre) will be meagre and thus advertising costs will be higher than necessary.

There are several yardsticks that can apply and no rule as to which is the most effective can be laid down, for individual companies must inevitably have their own special problems.

One method of obtaining the overall ratio is:

$$\frac{\text{Cost of recruiting}}{\text{Average salaries of new intake}}$$

provided this is, if applicable, broken down into different categories of recruitment. Advertising each week for secretaries and storekeepers might show a far lower ratio (higher costs) if during the course of the year three top-level executives had to be sought, using a large technical personnel agency and perhaps paying the costs of the interviews of potential recruits from abroad. So when applying the above formula care must be taken to "adjust to the unusual".

But the normal wastage in recruitment is usually considered by the personnel department as best instanced by the ratios

$$\frac{\text{Number of advertisements}}{\text{Average number of replies}}$$

and/or

$$\frac{\text{Cost of advertisements}}{\text{Number of successful applicants}}$$

If there are several different methods of recruitment then advertising must be clarified as a percentage of the remaining methods, and again this can be related to success and costs.

Suppose that (a) total cost of recruitment is £15,000 per annum and (b) advertising costs are £10,000 per annum

$$\frac{£10,000 \times 100}{£15,000} = 67\%$$

Advertising accounts for 67% of total recruitment costs.

If you realised that advertising was responsible for 90% of the successful candidates recruited, it would be clear that the costs of the remaining methods should be carefully scrutinised.

Newspaper advertising

If you book a page in two newspapers for a fortnight your number of advertisements would be $2 \times 5 \times 2 = 20$ (five days per week issue).

If as a result you received 120 replies, with no breakdown as to source, then 20/120 gives a ratio of 0·17 for that particular fortnight. But here the easier designation is 1/ratio = 1/0·17, *i.e.* 6 to 1 meaning six replies from one advertisement.

If another series of advertisements resulted in a ratio of 0·10, then reasons should be sought—such as the way in which the original advertisement was drafted, the time of year, holiday periods, a neighbouring company cutting back during the first series, and so on. Analysis is valueless unless underlying reasons for the results are studied with a view to future action.

Cost of recruiting through advertisements
Suppose the 20 advertisements cost £400 in all. Therefore

$$\frac{\text{Cost of advertisements}}{\text{Replies}} = \frac{£400}{120}$$

$$= £3·34 \text{ cost per reply}$$

Suppose out of the 120 replies, 75 candidates were successful. Then

$$\frac{\text{Cost of advertisements}}{\text{Successful candidates}} = \frac{£400}{75}$$

$$= £5·34 \text{ cost per successful candidate}$$

Incidentally the percentage of successful candidates against replies was either

$$\frac{75 \times 100}{120}$$

or

$$\frac{3·34 \times 100}{5·34} = 62\tfrac{1}{2}\%$$

Cost of recruiting through agencies
Another firm, in a large city for instance, might well prefer to obtain their secretaries and office staff entirely through agencies, keeping advertisements for their operatives and warehouse staff.

Here the breakdown costs will best be related to the monthly invoices for agencies:

Period	Agency A Costs	Recruits	Agency B Costs	Recruits	Agency C Costs	Recruits
1	£75	25	£20	4	£10	3
2	£50	20	£30	6	£20	4
3	£100	15	£50	15	£20	5
	£225	60	£100	25	£50	12
	225/60 = £3·75		100/25 = £4		50/12 = £4·17	

The above analysis is valueless unless there is "comment" by the personnel officer. Obviously Agency A is slightly "cheaper" overall, at first glance, but period 3 shows an unusually high cost against recruits received. Were some of the recruits dissatisfied after a week's work and left, and had to be replaced by the agency? Did Agency A choose badly in the first place? The other agencies, with no very marked dissimilarities, were slightly more expensive. Is it that although their costs were higher they took more trouble to suit the firm's requirements? With these thoughts in mind the personnel selection officer should send for the relevant files and investigate. He might find that all the girls recruited for employment in the typing pool had a considerably higher turnover than the more senior secretaries. Could working conditions in the typing pool be improved? Were the agencies telling all the girls that they were being recruited for the "boss's secretary" when in the event they found themselves in the typing pool?

Recruiting costs at £ per head per year

If over the year (245 working days) recruitment costs were £15,000 and the number of recruits was 1000 over a 4-month period (87 working days), the cost per head in the 4-month period can be found as follows:

$$\frac{\text{Recruitment cost}}{\text{Successful applicants}} \times \frac{\text{No. of working days in period under review}}{\text{No. of working days in year}}$$

$$\frac{£15,000}{1000} \times \frac{87}{245} = £5{\cdot}33$$

which is a little different to the "first-glance" assessment by incorrectly calculating £15,000 total for 12 months and considering £5000 as the cost average over 4 months (£15,000 × 4/12 = £5000/1000 = £5 per head cost).

It is worth remembering therefore that advertising costs, recruitment costs and training costs should, rightly, all be considered on a days worked per year/days worked per period basis for departmental costing analysis. The Profit and Loss Account will naturally be on an annual basis as is usual.

Training costs

The basic ratio is

$$\frac{\text{Training costs}}{\text{Average no. of employees}}$$

and this ratio is set off by three main factors in keeping costs to a minimum:

(a) $$\frac{\text{Training costs}}{\text{Trainee days}}$$

(b) $$\frac{\text{Trainee days}}{\text{Trainees}}$$

(c) $$\frac{\text{Trainees}}{\text{Total no. of employees}}$$

Costs can be reduced by increasing the number of trainees under training in (a), reducing the number of days' training in (b) and assessing carefully the right ratio of recruits under training in (c).

Too few recruits may cause bottlenecks if there is a sudden unexpected turnover, or if there are too few required in the recruitment pool the cause may be that promotion of those already on the staff is too slow. Too many recruits for jobs available could be caused initially by inaccurate selection and/or too many vacant jobs to be filled, *i.e.* something wrong somewhere causing a high rate of personnel turnover.

The mathematics for the ratios and percentages are quite normal and the same as in the previous section for recruiting costs/applicants, etc., remembering of course, where applicable, to relate the ratios to days worked per year/days worked per period.

Personnel turnover

In short, it is no good recruiting, spending much time and money on training, for the trainee to leave the firm shortly afterwards.

Analysis by the personnel officer must show departures by the length of time after training they take place, for if this period was short all the firm is doing is to train someone for another firm's benefit. Here conditions of service and promotion possibilities need to be carefully reviewed. If the time lag between final recruitment training and departure is, say, 3 years and turnover at this period of time is frequent the cause must be found.

To find the percentage personnel turnover, the following formula should be used:

$$\frac{\text{Number of employees leaving in period} \times 100}{\text{Average no. of employees in period}}$$

For example, in a company with an average number of 300 employees, 60 leave in one year. What is the percentage personnel turnover?

$$\frac{60 \times 100}{300} = 20\%$$

Industrial relations

No one can teach a firm industrial relations, for these are made up of so many human considerations such as understanding and the sympathetic and intelligent use of all employees at whatever level.

But purely mathematically the personnel department will have several yardstick ratios. Perhaps the most vital one, the key to which every other related ratio will probably be referred, is:

$$\frac{\text{Personnel costs}}{\text{Average no. of employees}}$$

We have already dealt with recruitment and training costs as ratios of recruits retained and the average number of employees respectively. A ratio that might be difficult to determine is:

$$\frac{\text{Costs of bad industrial relations}}{\text{Average no. of employees}}$$

Everyone's view of bad industrial relations will doubtless vary widely but whatever they are this ratio should be valued as a "loss of profits". You cannot value against sales, for a short, quick stoppage may not noticeably affect sales, or if it did there might be a considerable time lag before it became reflected in the sales ratios.

Strikes, working to rule, go-slow stoppages, unofficial holidays, an excessive amount of minor sickness are the factors which affect profits and which management must combat by good industrial relations.

Two ratios useful for purposes of comparison with our key ratio above are:

$$\frac{\text{Cost of production lost by bad industrial relations}}{\text{Average no. of employees}}$$

and

$$\frac{\text{Cost of excessive wage increases in excess of norm}}{\text{Average no. of employees}}$$

Other ratios which the personnel officer should have freely available are:

$$\frac{\text{No. of working days per head lost through } \begin{cases} \text{Strikes} \\ \text{Stoppages} \\ \text{Absenteeism} \\ \text{Sickness} \end{cases}}{\text{Average no. of employees}}$$

In each case, where relevant, working days/period days could be included.

Excessive wage claims cost a company an extra £50,000 per year and the average number of employees is 20,000 (all employees do not benefit from the wage claim).

Days worked throughout the year are 245 and the period under review is 6 months (in which there were only 4 national holidays), and thus 126 working days. (365 days less weekends = 260. 260/2 = 130 − 4 = 126.)

To find the additional cost per head, in the period, the formula is:

$$\frac{\text{Amount of wage claim}}{\text{Average no. of employees}} \times \frac{\text{No. of working days in period}}{\text{No. of working days in year}}$$

$$\frac{£50{,}000}{20{,}000} \times \frac{126}{245} = £1{\cdot}29 \text{ per head cost}$$

Absenteeism used to be shown on a per head basis. During the period under review (6 months), 5 days were lost and 7000 men were absent each day on average (one particular section of the workforce). The whole workforce numbered 20,000 and so absenteeism involved 35% of the total.

To find the percentage of man days lost in the period, the following formula can be used:

$$\frac{\text{Man days lost}}{\text{Man days worked}} \times 100$$

$$\frac{(7000 \times 5) \times 100}{7000 \times 126} = 3\cdot 97\%$$

To find the percentage of man days lost in 6 months by the whole firm:

$$\frac{(7000 \times 5) \times 100}{20{,}000 \times 126} = 1\cdot 39\%$$

You could of course have found your 1·39% by taking 35% of 3·97%, but calculating percentages of percentages can often result in errors and the calculation should always be worked in full, as above.

Productivity agreements

The permutations connected with this topic are so vast that it would be valueless to enlarge on the variations. However, a simple example may give the reader food for thought and show how the stages of the mathematics can be calculated.

A small factory workforce is turning out machine parts on a basis of 130 parts per week, a 10-hour day and a 5-day week. For this each man is paid 50p per hour.

A productivity agreement suggests that the men increase their production by $15\frac{1}{2}\%$ but that they will work only 9 hours a day and want more pay. Management is prepared to accept provided there is no increased cost. Is it viable? What increase of wages is possible?

Stage 1. Find the part-cost per 10-hour day.

130 parts wage cost at 10×50p $= 500$p per day
1 part wage cost at $10 \times 50/130 = 3\cdot 85$p per part per day

Stage 2. A $15\frac{1}{2}\%$ increase in productivity means

$130 + (130 \times 15\cdot 5/100)\ 130 + 20 = 150$ parts per day

150 parts wage cost at $\dfrac{9 \times x}{150}$ = Part cost (to remain as previously because management refuses higher costs)

Stage 3. If we equate past with future in cost proportions we should be able to find x, which is the rate per hour per unit cost:

$$\frac{10 \times 50}{130} \text{ must equal } \frac{9 \times x}{150}$$

therefore

$$x = \frac{10 \times 50 \times 150}{130 \times 9}$$
$$= 64 \cdot 10$$
$$= 64\text{p}$$

Stage 4. Check:

$$130 \text{ parts } \frac{10 \times 50}{130} = 3 \cdot 85\text{p day parts/cost}$$

$$150 \text{ parts } \frac{9 \times 64}{100} = 3 \cdot 85\text{p day parts/cost}$$

Therefore the cost per day turnover has not increased and the men are working 9 hours a day instead of 10 hours. The men will receive 64p per hour instead of 50p as previously. Therefore for 5 days a week, 9 hours a day, they will have a gross weekly wage of £0·64 × 9 × 5 = £28·80, whereas previously they had £0·50 × 10 × 5 = £25.

In fact 100 more parts are machined per week for 5 hours' less work and a gross wage increase of £3.80 per week. There is no increased cost to the company, for the increase in wages is recovered from increased turnover.

If only the solution to all productivity problems was as simple as this.